STOWE
LANDSCAPE
GARDENS

THE NATIONAL TRUST

CONTENTS

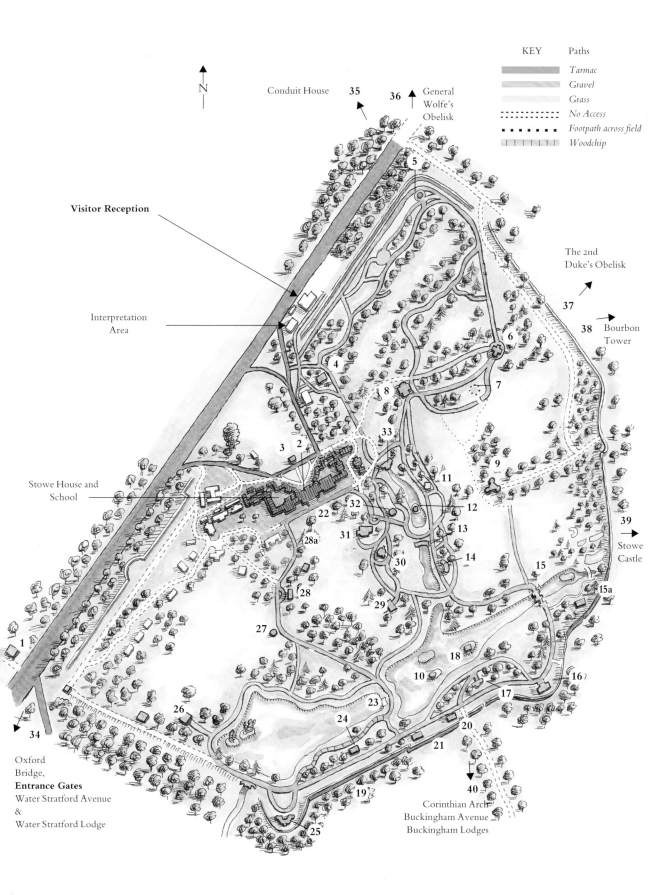

N

Conduit House **35** **36** General
Wolfe's
Obelisk

Visitor Reception

5

The 2nd
Duke's Obelisk

Interpretation
Area

6 **37**

38 Bourbon
Tower

4

7

8

33

3 **2**

9

Stowe House and
School

11

32 **12**

22 **13**

31

28a **30** **14**

39
Stowe
Castle

28 **15**

15a

29

27 **18**

1 **10**

16

17

26 **23**

24 **20**

34 **19** **21**

40

Oxford
Bridge,
Entrance Gates **25**
Water Stratford Avenue
&
Water Stratford Lodge

Corinthian Arch
Buckingham Avenue
Buckingham Lodges

KEY   Paths

Tarmac
Gravel
Grass
No Access
Footpath across field
Woodchip

CHAPTER ONE

THE MEANING OF STOWE

Visitors to Stowe sometimes ask, understandably enough, where the flower gardens are, and it has to be explained that Stowe is not that kind of garden. Though there are a few formal flower-beds within the balustrade on the south side of the house, all beyond is a picture of idealised nature, whose elements are grass and trees and water, with buildings carefully sited to give accents to the view and allow the wandering eye a resting place. An equally important question is 'What does the garden mean?' But that is a question which visitors hardly ever ask, for the concept that a garden as large as Stowe could have a specific and detailed programme of meaning – a sort of philosophic or political manifesto on the ground – is alien to our way of thinking. Yet it has been a controlling principle in some of the great gardens of the past. The Roman emperor Hadrian followed it at Tivoli. So did the creators of several gardens in Renaissance Italy, and the idea was taken up in eighteenth-century England, at Stourhead in Wiltshire, for example. Nowhere, however, was the garden programme more elaborate and detailed than at Stowe.

The family who created it were eighteenth-century Whigs, conscious descendants of the men whose opposition to the absolutist ambitions of the Stuart monarchy in the previous century had culminated in the Glorious Revolution of 1688. As a result, they could claim to have established constitutional monarchy and political freedom in England, and they saw themselves as the chosen defenders of liberty. Throughout the eighteenth century, the proprietors of Stowe and their relations were steadfast, if independent, adherents of the Whig cause, even to their own political disadvantage, and, as John Martin Robinson remarks, this allegiance 'runs through the garden architecture like a leitmotif'.

Viscount Cobham began in very much the same way as Marlborough's other generals returning home after the war with France came to an end in 1713. He laid out formal gardens, in which the walks and cross-walks were terminated by buildings and monuments, with all the conventional garden furniture. Early on, he demonstrated his loyalty to the new, and none too secure, Hanoverian regime by setting up an equestrian statue of George I, and this was followed by statues of the Prince and Princess of Wales (later George II and Queen Caroline), a special compliment being paid to Caroline, whose statue was sited directly facing that of Venus in the Rotondo, so that princess and goddess seemed to gaze at each other as equals. This can perhaps be seen as mere political flattery, but as the gardens departed from strict symmetry, expanding southwards and westwards during the 1720s to embrace Home Park within a perimeter walk, an astonishing variety of idiosyncratic and evocative buildings was added: a temple of honour surrounded by the busts of eight British 'worthies', a miniature villa in the latest Palladian taste, statues of the seven Saxon gods who gave their names to the days of the week, a memorial pyramid to Cobham's friend Sir John Vanbrugh, a hermitage with a 'ruined' turret, and so on. They were described in the topographical poem *Stowe* by Gilbert West, Cobham's nephew, published in 1732, and it is clear from this poem that up to that date, though the physical layout of the garden followed an artistic design, the ideas had been added piecemeal as an afterthought in no coherent order. From 1733, however, when a new area on the eastern side was taken into the garden, the programme of ideas was conceived as an organic part of the whole. The British Worthies, for example, were brought across into the Elysian Fields not only as a focus of the pictorial design, but also as a key piece in the iconographical theme.

The statue of George I was intended to demonstrate Viscount Cobham's loyalty to the new Hanoverian regime

The origin of the new garden was almost certainly an essay by Joseph Addison in the *Tatler* (No. 123, 21 January 1710), describing an allegorical dream. After falling asleep, Addison relates that he found himself in a huge wood, which had many paths and was full of people. He joined a group of middle-aged men marching 'behind the standard of Ambition', and describes the route he took and the buildings he saw. The essential features of the Elysian Fields are all there: a long straight path (the Great Cross Walk at Stowe) was terminated by a temple of virtue (Ancient Virtue), beyond which (over the river) lay a temple of honour (British Worthies); nearby was a ruinous temple of vanity (Modern Virtue). The classes of people mentioned in the dream, and the effigies too, correspond to the

statues actually set up in the gardens. So it seems beyond doubt that Addison's essay provided the programme which was to be illustrated by the architect and garden designer. Since William Kent was then acting in both these capacities, the decorative buildings and the garden setting must have come from his hand. But the iconography would have been worked out by Gilbert West and the other literary members of Cobham's circle. Very likely Alexander Pope, himself an enthusiastic gardener and frequent house-guest at Stowe, had a share in it.

When they came to select heroic figures for the Temple of Ancient Virtue, it was to Greece they turned rather than Rome, for the record of imperial Roman tyranny recalled French and Stuart despotism too strongly. Homer, Socrates and Epaminondas were there as the greatest poet, philosopher and soldier of the Ancient World; all three had been chosen by Pope in 1711 to fill the same positions in his poem *The Temple of Fame*. The fourth was the law-giver Lycurgus, who was believed to have established in Sparta the balanced constitution of limited monarchy so much admired by eighteenth-century Whigs.

The same theme was continued on the other side of the valley in the Temple of British Worthies, which contained the sixteen members of the British nation worthy to be seen in the same company. The eight men of contemplation included poets, scientists and philosophers like Shakespeare, Milton, Newton and Locke, all 'thinkers' revered by the Whig establishment, especially the last of these. For in his *Second Treatise of Government* (1690) Locke had provided the philosophic justification for the Glorious Revolution. The eight men of action were mostly statesmen and soldiers from recent English history, heroes who had fought, and in some cases died, in the struggle against the Stuarts, men like Sir Walter Ralegh and John Hampden, and, most importantly, William III. From their situation beside the stream the British Worthies looked up – literally and metaphorically – at their heroic Greek exemplars in the Temple of Ancient Virtue, who were thus offered as models for any contemporary Englishman ambitious to serve his country.

All these features were in accord with an ideal

The Temple of British Worthies celebrates figures of thought and action revered by the Whigs

Whig vision of government. But between the conception of the programme and its detailed execution Cobham fell out with the Prime Minister, Sir Robert Walpole, over the Excise Bill in 1733, was dismissed from his regiment, and joined other prominent Whigs in Opposition. The political platform of these self-styled 'Patriots' was the traditional Whig defence of liberty and the constitution, which, they claimed, were being cynically destroyed by Walpole's policy of systematic corruption in Parliament. Their campaign was concentrated against Walpole himself, but by implication, though it could only be hinted at, they were also opposing George II. They took as their figurehead Frederick, Prince of Wales, who had quarrelled with his father and set up an independent court, and before long another of Cobham's nephews, George Lyttelton, became the Prince's secretary. So in the gardens of Stowe, now a hotbed of Patriot opposition, the simple philosophic statement was overlaid with a political manifesto.

This shift in Cobham's political position explains the selection of the only two Worthies from earlier English history, King Alfred and Edward, Prince of Wales, better known to us as the Black Prince. Alfred, who, according to his inscription, 'crush'd corruption, guarded liberty, and was the founder of the English constitution', embodied the same theme as Lycurgus. But he was also there, no less importantly, as an ironic statement of everything that George II was not. And *Edward*, Prince of Wales was a thin disguise for *Frederick*, who the Patriots hoped would take Alfred as model rather than George when he became King, and would 'preserve his natural gentleness and modesty ... in the height of glory and fortune', like the Black Prince. Inscriptions above other Worthies contained similar messages which were an invitation to read between the lines, but the most obvious, and curious, item of this Patriot manifesto was the adaptation of Addison's temple of vanity. The Temple of Ancient Virtue, with its four heroic figures from Greek Antiquity, was described as being 'in a very flourishing condition', in contrast with the Temple of Modern Virtue nearby, which was built as a ruin, with a headless statue inside, as a satirical comment on the degraded state of contemporary public life.

After Frederick had paid an ostentatious visit to Stowe in 1737, the political theme became more explicit. Next to be developed was Hawkwell Field, the eastern area of the garden, and the Temple of Friendship was built at its southern end to house the busts of the Patriots, now quite openly including Frederick. On the ceiling was an allegorical picture of Britannia with three figures; two of them proudly displayed scrolls recording British achievements in the reigns of Edward III and Elizabeth, whereas the name on the scroll of the third – presumed to be George II – was 'cover'd with her Mantle' in shame. This was an attack on what the Patriots saw as Walpole's weak foreign policy, jeopardising Britain's trade. The Palladian Bridge nearby, which was built with a blank wall on its eastern side, further illustrated the mercantile theme of Whig policy. Paintings of Ralegh and William Penn, two of Britain's colonial pioneers, were placed at either end, and between them was a sculpted relief of the four continents bringing their products to Britannia, a demonstration of the close links between Whig politicians and City merchants. At the northern end of the vista stood the Queen's Temple, the domain of Lady Cobham, decorated with murals of ladies employed in shell work and other pursuits appropriate to their sex – not meddling, as Queen Caroline had, in politics, which should be the business of men. Set high on the hill between the Queen's Temple and the Temple of

The Gothic Temple was the climax of Lord Cobham's 'political gardening'

Friendship, and thus visible from many corners of the estate, was the Gothic Temple, the climax of Cobham's political gardening.

'Gothic' conveys little more to us now than an architectural style, but to the eighteenth century it was, like 'Goth', a word of potent meaning. Assumed to be synonymous with 'Germanic' (as 'Goth' was with 'Jute'), it suggested the vigour, hardihood and love of liberty of those tough northern tribes who conquered Rome, in contrast with the spineless servility of the Latin peoples. It was believed too that the democratic procedures which Tacitus had described as typical of Germanic assemblies had been brought over to England by Saxon (or Jutish) invaders, so that England's mixed government was often referred to as 'our old Gothick Constitution'. Furthermore, the Reformation could be regarded as the North's rescuing of humanity, for the second time, from the decadence and tyranny of the Roman South. So 'Gothic' came to imply an amalgam of all these moral and cultural values, and no building could better have summed up the Whig vision or Patriot protest. The Gothic Temple was dedicated specifically 'To the Liberty of our Ancestors'. Round it were placed the seven Saxon Deities, transported from the western side of the gardens; on the ceiling of its dome were painted the arms of Cobham's Saxon forebears; and over the door he placed a fine Gothic inscription from Corneille's play *Horace* (1639), which may be translated thus: 'I thank the Gods that I am not a Roman.' Implied was the second line of the couplet: 'So as to keep some human feelings still.'

Before the Gothic Temple was completed, Walpole fell from power, and once the common enemy had gone, the Patriot alliance crumbled, discrediting sections of the garden programme. Horace Walpole, the Prime Minister's son, who visited in 1770, protested that he had 'no patience at building and planting a satire', and he was right about the folly of erecting monuments on the shifting sands of a political manifesto. But Cobham's original plan of presenting an ideal political vision through the buildings, statues and inscriptions of a garden was surely a noble concept, and enough still survives of his extraordinary sermon in stone to intrigue, and perhaps challenge, an open-minded visitor.

CHAPTER TWO

DESCRIPTION OF THE GARDEN

VISITOR ROUTE

In the eighteenth and nineteenth centuries, the public would arrive from the Buckingham direction and begin their tour at the Bell Gate. Those guests of the family who have left written descriptions generally begin with the house and describe the garden starting with the south steps. But no other garden was enlarged and developed so continuously over such a long period as Stowe, and no standard route for visitors has ever become established. This guide therefore describes each of the principal areas into which the garden can be divided, the surviving garden buildings, which are numbered for recognition on the plan on pp. 2–3, and the most important of those now lost (in square brackets).

THE APPROACHES

THE BUCKINGHAM LODGES

The Grand Avenue does not seem to have been furnished with lodges until about 1805, and it is not known who designed them. All their ornaments – the chimneys formed as antique altars, the balusters and the relief tablets – are in Coade stone bearing marks for the period 1799–1813. Until the practice of grazing the Grand Avenue was abandoned in the twentieth century, the lodges had wooden gates.

THE GRAND AVENUE

The avenue is one and a half miles long (the overall distance from the Buckingham Lodges to the south portico is more than three miles). The original trees were elms, but with beech substituted in the depressions to give variety of form. The undulations of the land heighten the drama of the approach: the effect of the first sight of the Corinthian Arch is aug-

mented by its subsequent disappearance, only to reappear with the clear lines of the south portico (still a mile away) now framed within it.

The house completed by Sir Richard Temple in 1683 was built to face the tower of the medieval church at Buckingham (see p. 21); its steeple was the only building that could be seen over the brow of the hill that lies between the house and the town. This axis remains fundamental, despite the rebuilding of the church in a new position in the 1770s.

Lord Cobham and Charles Bridgeman sent out an avenue on this line from a rampart at the southern edge of the Octagon Lake to the summit of the hill. This was removed when Earl Temple threw open the South Vista in the 1760s. He began planting the new avenue to Buckingham in about 1774.

At the time of the great sale in 1921, the Grand Avenue was lotted into building plots, but was privately bought by Clough Williams-Ellis, the architect employed by the newly founded school. It was purchased from him in 1924 with funds donated by Old Etonians as a 'christening present' to Stowe. Because of Dutch elm disease the avenue had to be completely replanted in the 1970s, with blocks of beech, lime and horse chestnut.

Today the road veers westwards at the foot of the incline to the Corinthian Arch, and remains outside the park boundary until it joins the Oxford Avenue. The highway runs roughly parallel with the line taken by Lord Temple's approach once it had reached the arch; at that point his guests would also have turned off the great axis and swept round the park on what was later called the Queen's Drive.

[THE CHACKMORE FOUNTAIN]

Halfway down the Grand Avenue, slightly to the north of the turning to Chackmore, stood the Chackmore Fountain, a tall brick kiosk incorporating a Gibbsian door surround and other early eighteenth-century stonework. A confection of the 1st Duke, it was erected *c.*1831 to mark the source of a spring which flows under the road. It later fell into disrepair and had to be dismantled in the late 1950s.

THE CORINTHIAN ARCH (40)

It was designed in 1765 for Earl Temple by his young cousin, Thomas Pitt, later Lord Camelford, to close the sublime vista newly opened from the south steps of the house, and completed in 1767, but when the Grand Avenue was extended southwards on the same axis eight years later, it served equally well to convince visitors that they were approaching a 'Top Seat' (Vanbrugh's term for Castle Howard). The arch also contains two houses, originally for keepers. It has windows in the side elevations.

The construction of the arch involved the craftsmen that Earl Temple was to employ on the completion of the south front – the mason Richard Batchelor and the sculptor James Lovell, who carved the Corinthian capitals and the swags of leaves on the parapet. The pair of flanking milliary (milestone) columns was added by the Marquess of Buckingham by 1780. In 2004, work was completed on the exterior of the arch, which involved repairs to the roof, exterior stonework, balustrade and stucco restoration. The work was generously financed by the late Miss M. R. Perrin.

THE OXFORD AVENUE AND THE COURSE

Although the approach from the Water Stratford Lodge to Stowe is less grand than the Grand Avenue from Buckingham (see p. 8), it exploits the terrain with equal skill. The lodge was designed by Edward Blore and built in 1843. The double avenue was probably first planted in the last years of the eighteenth century. It roughly followed the line of the Roman road from Bicester to Towcester, which did not survive in use at this point, but remained significant as a boundary. The avenue drives straight ahead over undulating farmland, crossing two streams and two public roads on its way to the Oxford Gates at the edge of the park. At this point it pauses, allowing wide views of the park and encouraging a slower progress (just as the Grand Avenue from Buckingham yields to open landscape at the Corinthian Arch). From the gates the drive continues straight as an arrow up to the Boycott Pavilions, which mark the edge of the gardens.

The Corinthian Arch

The Oxford Gates; engraving by T. Medland

The drive then runs along what is known as the Course, established in 1712 with borders of grazed turf defined by two rows of trees. On the right the ha-ha runs parallel to the Course along the edge of the gardens.

THE OXFORD GATES

The entrance to the park from the south-west is marked by a screen of railings flanked by pavilions. There are coats of arms on both sides of the central piers; those on the east (inner) side are the arms of Earl Temple, who erected the screen here in 1761, carved in stone; they were probably originally on the outer side but were supplanted in 1787 by those of Earl Temple's nephew and successor, by then Marquess of Buckingham; these were executed in Coade stone. The piers and screens were originally designed in 1731 by William Kent for a position further to the north-east (see p. 11). The pavilions at either end were probably added by Vincenzo Valdrè in the 1780s. The original ironwork of the main gates was removed for the war effort in the 1940s; in a nice reversal, their recent reinstatement by David Renwick following photographs of *c.* 1900 made use of wrought iron salvaged from the anchor of a German battleship scuttled in Scapa Flow.

THE OXFORD BRIDGE AND WATER (34)

Earl Temple's grand new approach from the direction of Oxford crossed the shallow valley of the stream running down from Dadford, presumably by means of a bridge but perhaps only by a ford. In the course of improving this part of the landscape, he dammed the river and extended what had been the millpond for a paper mill to form a serpentine lake. The bridge at its centre, perhaps designed by Earl Temple himself and built in 1761, is ornamented by two sets of four urns; those on the centre of the bridge were carved in the 1760s by Edward Batchelor, but the four at the ends were probably salvaged from the Sleeping Parlour (see p. 20), which Vanbrugh had probably designed for Cobham's garden.

THE BOYCOTT PAVILIONS (1)

James Gibbs's drawing for the two buildings on the brow of the hill overlooking the course of the stream is inscribed 'Design for two Pavilions at *Stow*

... within the one is an Octagon Room ... the other ... a Dwelling-house for a Gentleman'. They are named after the hamlet of Boycott, which lies about half-way down the Oxford Avenue. The first of them, to the east of the drive, was built by 1728; its arches were then open, and like the Rotunda it formed a belvedere across the Western Garden. It once contained lead statues in niches of Cicero, Marcus Aurelius, Livia and Faustina. The western pavilion was added a year or two later to accommodate the 'gentleman' referred to on the drawing; he was Col. Samuel Speed, one of Lord Cobham's comrades-in-arms.

The pair of pavilions marked the entrance to the gardens from the park, standing on the line of Bridgeman's ha-ha, and they were linked in the mid-1730s by the railing and gate-piers designed by Kent which now stand at the entrance to the park some distance to the south-west (see p. 10). As designed by Gibbs, they had stone pyramid roofs (echoing Vanbrugh's demolished great pyramid, which stood within view; see p. 16), but these were

replaced in 1758 by the present domes, designed by Giovanni Battista Borra.

The open eastern pavilion was converted into a house by Stowe School in 1952.

[NELSON'S SEAT]

This small temple, described in the 1745 Seeley guidebook as 'an airy Recess to the North-West of the House, from whence there is an open Prospect', was built to the designs of Sir John Vanbrugh in 1719–20. It took the form of a columned recess flanked by two large piers, surmounted by gadrooned urns. Although dedicated by Lord Cobham to Vanbrugh's memory, it was generally known as 'Nelson's Seat' – after William Nelson, the foreman responsible for its construction rather than the Victor of the Nile. In 1773 it was extensively recast and given a new façade in the form of a Doric portico. Nelson's Seat was demolished before 1797 and today only a grassy mound behind the School cricket pavilion marks its site.

The Oxford Bridge and Water, with one of the Boycott Pavilions on the horizon

THE STATUE OF KING GEORGE I (3)

When one approached the house from the west in Lord Cobham's time, the view along the Course was centred on the equestrian statue of George I in the guise of the Emperor Marcus Aurelius, which now stands nearer the front of the house. It was cast in lead in 1723 by Andries Carpentière (Andrew Carpenter) and C. Burchard, and served to celebrate Lord Cobham's return to political favour after the death of Queen Anne. It was to George I that he owed his title of Viscount (1718) and the restitution of his military command, which enabled him to profit handsomely from the Vigo expedition in 1719. It was moved to its present position by 1797 and restored by the Trust in 2002.

THE NORTH FRONT (2)

Some of Lord Cobham's profits were devoted to the modernisation of the north front of his father's increasingly old-fashioned house. The front as it now appears probably corresponds well with Cobham's original intentions, but much of it dates from well after his time. It is arranged around a *cour d'honneur*, and in a letter written by Vanbrugh to his employer at Castle Howard, the Earl of Carlisle, there is evidence of its continental inspiration. He urges Lord Carlisle against a central gateway to the forecourt there, recommending an approach at right-angles to the house:

My Lord Cobham is mightily for this Expedient, and tells me he has seen the very thing done, to a Great Palace in Germany, and had, he thought, an Admirable good effect, the plain Wall in the Front looking with a bolder air of Defence than if there had been a Gate through it.

Unlike Lord Carlisle or the Duke of Marlborough, Lord Cobham already had a substantial house, which can still readily be distinguished as the eleven central bays of this front. His modifications, which date from the mid-1720s, were the raising of a parapet roof with 'towers' to the corners in place of the earlier hipped outline, the removal of the cupola and the addition of a giant Ionic portico. To either side were added stables and other out-offices, and the court was formalised with screen walls. Vanbrugh's part in these changes is uncertain; while the portico has been attributed to him, only the out-offices (including an orangery at the western end) are certainly his.

The north front

At each side of the forecourt are two pairs of arches. Those in line with the house are the earliest and were designed by Kent in the 1730s as entrances to the service yards. The arches at right-angles to these were designed as entrances to the garden by Giacomo Leoni in about 1740.

It was only in the 1770s that the forecourt was completed by Earl Temple with the addition of the colonnades, curving out from the house to the line of Kent's arches (which were incorporated at this point into high screen walls). He also added the Coade stone lions flanking the steps to the portico, which were supplied in 1778.

THE HA-HA (19)

Charles Bridgeman (d. 1738) was in charge of Lord Cobham's gardening activities from c.1715 until c.1733. His achievement was in taking what was already a notable and fashionable garden to a new level of grandeur, vastly extending its boundaries and establishing the great lines and vistas which in every direction dictated the development of the garden for a hundred years.

Stowe was Bridgeman's first major work. He had begun his career as a landscape designer with Henry Wise, Vanbrugh and Stephen Switzer at Blenheim, and although he subsequently worked for the King, his own opinion of his work for Lord Cobham was such that he commissioned in 1733 from Jacques Rigaud a series of fifteen views, which were published by his widow Sarah in 1739.

Bridgeman was credited by Horace Walpole with the invention of the ha-ha, but in fact it originated in the previous century, and in France (for example, at the Grand Trianon at Versailles), and although Bridgeman's Stowe ha-ha was probably the longest ever built, it did not achieve the whole trick. It was not invisible, as the wall rose a few feet above the level of the walk behind it, as can be seen on the right-hand side of Rigaud's *View of the Queen's Theatre from the Rotunda* (illustrated on p. 14).

Bridgeman's ha-has at Stowe and at Blenheim, with their terrace walks and above all their bastions at the corners, bear a closer relation to military fortification than to the unification of pasture and lawn achieved by the same device by Kent at Rousham (and here at Stowe, once the low walls were razed). In both places he was working for

soldiers, who had seen at first hand the fortifications of Louis XIV's great military engineer Sébastien Le Prestre de Vauban. The vertical face of the Stowe ha-ha was formed as a stockade, revetted with turf.

THE HOME PARK

This area was first taken into the garden in about 1720 by Lord Cobham. The Home Park was an area of *ferme ornée* (now part of Stowe's golf course) enclosed by a terrace walk and the Eleven-Acre Lake. The temples and monuments in this part of the garden shared the theme of Love – not romantic love, but illicit and frustrated love.

[THE QUEEN'S THEATRE]

This is now little more than an expanse of grass, but it once united several of the most important features in the western part of the gardens. Created by Lord Cobham in 1721, it consisted of grass terraces and a rectangular canal stretching at right-angles from the centre of the South Vista west to the Rotunda, and is best recorded in its heyday in Rigaud's *View of the Queen's Theatre from the Rotunda*, published as an engraving in 1739.

Several of the axial views included in Rigaud's print have disappeared. The elaborate terraces and canal reverted to a gentle grass hollow in 1762–4, when the statue of Queen Caroline and its quadruple pedestal (see p. 15) were moved west of the Rotunda. The Guglio or fountain (see p. 24) on the far right was removed from the Octagon Lake in mid-century, and Nelson's Seat, which appears to the far left (Rigaud has compressed 120 degrees into 90), was demolished before 1797.

THE ROTUNDA (27)

Shift now the closer Scene: and view around,
With various Beauties the wide Landskip crown'd....
Lo! in the Centre of this beauteous Scene,
Glitters beneath her Dome the Cyprian Queen.

Gilbert West, *Stowe* (1732)

Designed by Vanbrugh and built in 1720–1, the Rotunda remains perhaps the most solemnly beautiful and eloquent of Lord Cobham's temples, particularly when seen across the Eleven-Acre Lake from the Temple of Venus. Its gilded occupant

View of the Queen's Theatre from the Rotunda;
*engraved by Jacques Rigaud c.1733–4, but not published
till 1739*

(the Venus de' Medici, the 'Cyprian Queen' of
West's poem, who was not only goddess of love,
but patroness of gardening) returned in replica
in 1998.

The importance of the Rotunda in Lord Cobham's first garden is clear from Bridgeman's
brilliant bird's-eye view, made in about 1719 (illustrated on pp. 14–15). Here, the point of view is not
the house, diminutive and distant, but the Rotunda,
which forms a sort of hub from which the main
lines of the garden radiate. With the westward
expansion of the garden in the 1720s, the enclosure
of the Home Park and the completion of the
'Garden of Love', this became even more important to the design.

Vanbrugh's hemispherical dome and finial were
replaced in 1752–4 by a lower, saucer-shaped dome
designed by Borra. Then in 1773–4 the masons

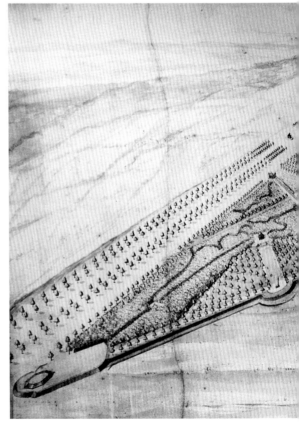

*(Right) Bridgeman's c.1719 bird's-eye view of the garden
shows the Rotunda as a key axis of the semi-formal design.
Note the straight lines of the Ha-Ha around the Home
Park in the foreground (Gough Drawings a.4, fol.46r,
Bodleian Library, Oxford)*

Richard Wyatt and Edward Batchelor were paid for 'working the Rotonda columns'. This further modification of Vanbrugh's original design may have been devised by Valdrè. The place of honour vacated at that time by Venus was given in 1777 to a figure of Bacchus, but this was removed in 1844 and sold in 1848.

STATUE OF QUEEN CAROLINE (26)

At the opposite end of the Queen's Theatre from the Rotunda, Lord Cobham raised a statue of Caroline of Ansbach, consort to George II, on a pedestal of four fluted Ionic columns, probably designed by Vanbrugh. It must date from just before the time of their accession in 1727. The statue was carved in Portland stone, probably by John Michael Rysbrack, who carved that of George II (see p. 16). Around the entablature of her pedestal was inscribed in gilded letters '*Honori, Laudi, Virtuti Divae Carolinae*' ('To the Honour, Praise and Virtue of the Divine Caroline'), as if to number her among the other deities of the garden. To strengthen this allusion, statues of shepherds and nymphs (probably in lead by Carpenter) were placed in the garden landscape around the base of her columns.

When Earl Temple felled his uncle's Abele Walk to widen the South Vista in 1762 (see p. 21), the Queen lost her woody backdrop, and it was unsatisfactory that she should present her rear view to his most important landscape composition. She and her columns were therefore moved to their present position near the western end of the Eleven-Acre Lake, displacing in the process what was then known as the Fane of Diana ('Gibbs's Building'), which was removed to the far eastern corner of the Grecian Valley and rechristened the Fane of Pastoral Poetry (see p. 50). Winding paths connected Caro-

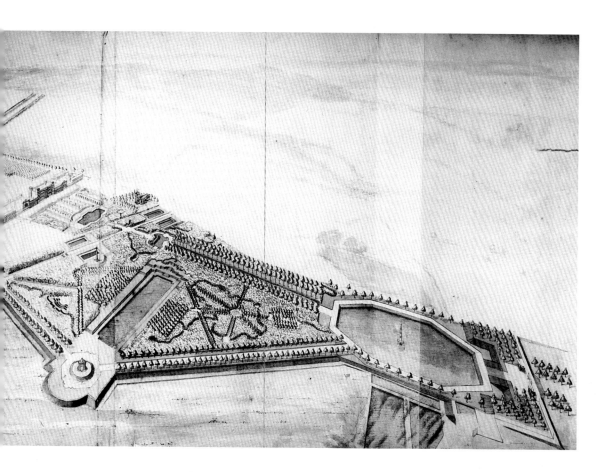

Statue of Queen Caroline

line to the Pyramid and the Boycott Pavilions, passing through 'cabinets' within the garden's perimeter belt.

STATUE OF KING GEORGE II (28a)

In 1724 Viscount Perceval described this statue of Queen Caroline's consort in his robes as Prince of Wales and raised on a single Corinthian column that 'overlooked, from a considerable height ... the Garden of Venus'. By the time Rigaud drew his view in 1733–4, it had been moved to a less promi-

nent position among the distant trees to the left of Queen Caroline's monument. Bearing in mind Cobham's antagonism towards the King, this was hardly surprising.

The King's column was dismantled soon after 1800 and not re-erected. His statue was repositioned in 1840 on the site of Nelson's Seat (see p. 11) by the north front, and sold in 1921. It is now at Port Lympne in Kent. A cast was made to be placed on the re-erected column in 2004.

Disposed amid the walks which ran along the northern margin of the Home Park was a further series of garden buildings and monuments, all since destroyed or moved elsewhere. Their sites are now largely occupied by the outlying buildings of Stowe School (no public access). They included:

[THE VANBRUGH PYRAMID]

An eminence on the north-west corner of the Home Park was the site of one of Lord Cobham's most striking creations at Stowe: the Egyptian or Vanbrugh Pyramid. Sixty feet high, this steeply stepped construction was erected, posthumously, to the designs of Sir John Vanbrugh in 1726 and became his monument at Stowe. It bore a Latin inscription, translated as: 'To the Memory of *Sir John Vanbrugh*, by whom several of the Buildings in these Gardens were designed, Lord *Cobham* hath erected this Pyramid.'

A lugubrious quotation from Horace could be read in the square chamber within the structure, which was entered beneath two massively rusticated doorcases on its southern and eastern sides.

The appearance of the Vanbrugh Pyramid is well known from Rigaud's engraved views of 1739, but the stonework of its precipitous flanks seems always to have given trouble. It was this which presumably led to its truncation in 1771 and its final demolition in 1797. Only the foundations of the Pyramid now mark its site, hidden beneath a grassy mound near the modern Field Houses (not accessible to the public).

[ST AUGUSTINE'S CAVE]

Further west, hidden in a thicket off Nelson's Walk, was a small rustic edifice with a thatched roof, described as 'a cell form'd of Moss and Roots of Trees interwoven, with a straw Couch in the Inside'.

Enlarging on the amorous theme of the other buildings around the Home Park, it contained three lewd inscriptions in 'Monkish Latin Verse' which chronicled the hermit-saint's drastic attempts to conquer lustful thoughts. A whimsical creation of the early 1740s, this flimsy root-house had disappeared by 1797.

[THE TEMPLE OF BACCHUS]

Nearby stood another lost Vanbrugh building, a 'Sumer hous' constructed of brick c.1718 and one of the first garden buildings at Stowe. A simple pedimented structure, it was later coated with stucco imitating coursed masonry and its interior was 'adorned with the *Revels of Bacchus*, painted by *Nollikins*', earning its dedication to the God of wine, drunkenness – and lechery. Further embellishments included two lead sphinxes, which appeared on the plinths flanking the doorway in 1768, and by 1797 the temple had become home to 'a large vase or fountain of blue marble with vine leaves and lions heads'. The Temple of Bacchus survived until 1926, when it was torn down to make way for Sir Robert Lorimer's new school chapel.

[COUCHER'S OBELISK]

A dwarf obelisk, erected before 1725, inscribed 'To the Memory of Robin Coucher', the Chaplain to Lord Cobham's regiment. A restless monument, it occupied at least two different sites beside the Home Park – including a spell in front of the Temple of Bacchus – before its expulsion in or about 1763.

[THE QUEEN OF HANOVER'S SEAT]

A clearing to the south-west of the Temple of Bacchus, a site in front of the present Roxburgh Hall, was the final resting place for the Saxon Altar, a large circular plinth scooped out to form seven seats. Once the focus of the circle of Saxon Deities, in their earliest (1727) incarnation off Nelson's Walk, it had been moved by 1744 to the Grecian Valley where it served as a base to a lead statue of the 'Dancing Faun' and was surrounded by a bevy of lead shepherds and shepherdesses. In 1843 it returned to the edge of the Home Park and, topped

with an urn and suitably inscribed, was rechristened the 'Queen of Hanover's Seat' in honour of a visit made in that year. The imposing hybrid was sold in the 1921 sale and it is now in a garden in Yorkshire.

THE TEMPLE OF VENUS (25)

The Temple of Venus stands on the southern bastion of Bridgeman's ha-ha overlooking the south end of the Eleven-Acre Lake. Dating from 1731, it marks the beginning of William Kent's employment in the gardens at Stowe, and the completion of the garden as it then existed. Even after Kent had contributed several more temples, it kept the alternative name of 'Kent's building'. It is built of Helmdon limestone and consists of a central pedimented block with an apsidal Ionic portico *in antis* linked to corner pavilions by arcaded quadrant walls. Apart from the central block, it has only one façade; the rear walls were rendered and for the most part hidden by shrubberies, which in the late eighteenth century consisted of a garden of evergreens.

No direct source for the design has been suggested. The careful siting of the building and the pronounced lean of the arcade piers were noticed by Thomas Whately in 1770, who observed that the 'elegant structure, inclined a little from a front view, becomes more beautiful by being thrown into perspective; and though at a greater distance, is more important than before, because it is alone in the view.'

Within the Temple of Venus the goddess was represented by a painting in the centre of the ceiling by the Venetian Francesco Sleter; the room was furnished with what was described as a 'pleasuring sopha', and inscribed around the frieze was the encouraging couplet from a Renaissance adaptation of the *Pervigilium Veneris*:

Nunc amet, qui nondum amavit;
Quique amavit, nunc amet.
(Let him love, who never lov'd before;
Let him who always lov'd, now love the more.)

The other parts of the decoration emphasised Venus's role in promoting sexual jealousy and strife. In the niches surrounding the portico were busts (copies recently reinstated) of the debauched emperors Nero and Vespasian and the adultresses Cleopatra and Faustina. The internal walls were

The Temple of Venus from across the Eleven-Acre Lake

once decorated with scenes from Spenser's *Faerie Queene*, also provided by Sleter. They told the story of Malbecco, the octagenarian husband of the seventeen-year-old Hellinore. She soon sought alternative pleasures, which were portrayed with frankness in the murals.

The stone domes to the pavilions collapsed before the end of the eighteenth century, and in 1827–8 the 1st Duke of Buckingham replaced them with pitched lead roofs. In 1827 the doorways were altered to form round-headed arches, but the recent restoration of the temple has reinstated Kent's design. Sleter's murals evidently perished or were painted over at the end of the eighteenth century and were replaced by the 1st Duke of Buckingham with a scheme of plain, pale-coloured walls bordered with wash lines in greenish blue.

The recent restoration has included the excavation of the ground to the south in order to reinstate the original line of the ha-ha. The shrubberies to either side have been replanted in the 'ranked' manner of the mid-eighteenth century according to available evidence, and beyond the ha-ha there now appears a scene Lord Cobham himself would have recognised: files of 'cased' tree seedlings on the lines of his original plantings, swinging round the bastion to link up with the earlier replantings on Warden Hill to the west.

[STATUE OF CAIN AND ABEL]

The significance of this lead group by Andrew Carpenter, which formerly stood on the sloping lawn in front of the Temple of Venus, was suggested in Samuel Boyse's poem *The Triumphs of Nature* (1742):

Thy temple, beauteous Venus, we survey'd;
Before, fit emblem of the lover's view,
Stand the first foes which nature ever knew;
Fit emblem, goddess, of thy cruel pow'r,
Which oft has bath'd the warring world in gore;
Has smil'd to set the dearest friends at strife,
And make the brother snatch the brother's life:
Yet mild at first, thy savage yoke appears,
And like this scene a beauteous prospect wears;
For scenes like this, thy fatal flame inspire,
Unnerve the soul – and kindle soft desire!

It was moved to the far end of the Grecian Valley in August 1765.

[COWPER'S URN]

A large stone urn with a wooden seat around its base was erected to the west of the Hermitage in 1827. It was sold in 1921 and its present whereabouts is unknown.

THE HERMITAGE (24)

Following the episode depicted by Sleter in the Temple of Venus, Malbecco took himself off to a cave in disgust, and close by the Temple of Venus is the rustic alcove known as the Hermitage, which may thus represent the last refuge of the misogynist. The planting was originally wild and rugged, incorporating many evergreens to reinforce the mood of melancholy.

The heavily rusticated and pedimented design of c.1731 is again by Kent and reappears in one of his own illustrations to an edition of Spenser's *Faerie Queene* published in 1751. In the pediment is a carving of pan-pipes in a wreath. One of its little turrets was built as a ruin, the first at Stowe and an early example. It was later renamed the Shepherd's Cove.

DIDO'S CAVE (28)

All but hidden in the shrubbery which surrounds it to the north of the Rotunda, Dido's Cave was probably built in the 1720s as a simple 'alcove'. It is not known who designed it.

The cave recalls the tragedy of the Queen of Carthage deserted by her lover Aeneas. In West's poem *Stowe* of 1732, it appears as 'The Randibus', to

which – seized by the sensation to which he is said to have given his name – the vicar of Stowe, the Rev. Conway Rand, pursued a 'frighted maid':

A Private Grotto promis'd safe Retreat:
Alas! too private, for too safely there
The fierce Pursuer seiz'd the helpless Fair;
The Fair he seiz'd, while round him all the Throng
Of laughing Dryads, Hymenaeals sung:
Pronubial Juno gave the mystick Sign,
And Venus nodded from her neighb'ring Shrine
    [ie the Rotunda].

West had paraphrased Virgil's account of Dido and Aeneas in his description of this incident. By 1738 the interior was decorated (probably by Sleter) with images of the tragic couple.

The façade is still partly covered with tufa, which was added for the Marchioness of Buckingham c.1781, at the same time as the Menagerie (see p. 21)

The Hermitage

was being built for her. Her son, the 1st Duke, made it her memorial by adding the inscription '*Mater Amata, Vale!*' ('Farewell, Beloved Mother') to the surviving inscription within, from *The Aeneid*: 'Speluncam Dido dux et Troianus eandem/ Deveniunt' ('Dido and the Trojan leader find their way to the cave').

[THE SLEEPING PARLOUR]

Hidden in the dense wilderness which separated the Home Park from the South Vista was the Sleeping Parlour or Temple of Sleep, probably by Vanbrugh and erected in 1725. Situated at the confluence of six paths, it was a square brick building with attached Ionic porticoes on two of its faces, one of which bore the tempting inscription '*cum Omnia sint in incerto, fave tibi*' ('Since all things are uncertain, indulge thyself'). The interior was decorated with

frescoes of 'the *Caesars* Heads, with several Festoons of Fruit and Flowers' and contained couches for weary visitors. It was demolished in 1760, but the extraordinary urns with sneering masks which formerly surmounted its parapet survive and now adorn the Oxford Bridge.

THE ARTIFICIAL RUINS (23)

The Eleven-Acre Lake is divided from the upper stretch of water known as the Octagon Lake by a causeway. Until recently this was far less open, shaded by tall trees that overhung the mass of rock-work constructed in the late 1730s and known in the earliest guides as the Artificial Ruins. As Seeley's 1750 engraving and several of Nattes's drawings show, it was intended to be seen from the lower ground to the west. It was a triple cascade, infested with small statues of nymphs and river gods, and

The Menagerie in 1914

incorporating at each side a vaulted boathouse. Earl Temple made further additions in 1751–8, and before 1797 obelisk-shaped urns with flame finials were placed at the ends of the ruins on the banks of the lake.

Artificial ruins tend to become more ruinous, and this cascade has twice been rebuilt. The first campaign was directed by the steward S. W. Savage in the late nineteenth century. They were again reconstructed in 1974. The planting has been reinstated as far as the Reservoirs Act permits on this artificial dam. It was intended to screen the Eleven-Acre Lake from the Octagon Lake and to extend the South Vista trees towards the Lake Pavilions.

[THE COLD BATH]

Nearby was the Cold Bath, a simple brick structure by Vanbrugh of about 1723, which was fed by waters from the Octagon Lake. It had disappeared by 1761.

THE MENAGERIE

It was built c.1781 on the northern side of the Lower Flower Garden south-west of the house by the 1st Marquess of Buckingham as a sort of *trianon* for his wife. It was probably designed by Valdrè, who also painted the ceiling of the central dome, over what was called Lady Buckingham's Sitting Room. The connecting quadrants served as orangeries, with aviaries in the pavilions at either end. The Menagerie became better known as a museum of stuffed animals. The 1st Duke of Buckingham acquired many of the curiosities from William Bullock's famous museum at 172 Piccadilly when it was sold in 1819, to which he added 10,000 geological specimens assembled by the Abbé Haüy and animal curiosities such as an eight-foot crocodile 'in the act of seizing a Tiger-cat', and 'a magnificent specimen of the Great Boa Constrictor, the largest ever seen in this country' (it measured 32 feet with a circumference of 30 inches). All of these specimens were dispersed in the 1848 sale. They must have constituted not only one of the greatest private museums in England but the most lavishly displayed, on gilt and marble-topped tables and stands.

Today the Lower Flower Garden is occupied by tennis courts.

THE SOUTH VISTA

The South Vista has been the principal axis of the garden since at least 1676, when Sir Richard Temple aligned the central entrance door of the south front to his new house with the spire of Buckingham church. He laid out terraced parterres below the south front and in 1682 a double avenue of white poplars known as the Abele Walk, which later connected the house with the Octagon Lake. Lord Cobham set up a series of lead statues by Van Nost of Apollo and the Nine Muses within niches cut into the flanking hedges. In the 1720s Bridgeman continued the avenue for Cobham with a further double avenue of beech trees from his ha-ha to the horizon. In the 1740s 'Capability' Brown flattened the parterres and removed the Van Nost statues to a site near the Doric Arch.

When Earl Temple inherited in 1749, the only trees of more than 40 years' standing were the poplars of the Abele Walk. They were considered an obstacle as early as 1742, when Defoe objected to the narrowness of the avenue. Twenty years later Lord Temple judged that the rest of the garden had grown sufficiently to admit the loss of these trees, and in the 1760s he embarked on what he immediately judged the 'finest alteration I ever made', the broadening and lengthening of the South Vista from the house.

The effect of his removal of the poplars and Bridgeman's avenue was itself a majestic extension of the landscape. By reshaping the Octagon Lake and removing the obelisk from it (parts of its masonry were reused as Wolfe's Obelisk), he lifted the eye to the further horizon and its grand new ornament, the Corinthian Arch, moving Vanbrugh's Doric Lake Pavilions further apart in the process.

The final ingredient in what must be one of the finest landscapes ever designed was the exploitation of light. The axis of the early garden had been set at some degrees east of south, and George Clarke has shown that, while there remained a continuous screen of foliage down the eastern (left-hand) side of the vista, the screen on the western side was pierced by Earl Temple to create with trees the effect of side-screens in a theatre:

On a sunny afternoon the cross-light adds depth to the landscape; but sometimes it does much more and

The South Vista from the Octagon Lake

creates a transcendent view of perfected nature – the epitome and model of the English Garden. No one who knows Stowe well can forget those still summer evenings when the sun picks out details on the Corinthian Arch and the Lake Pavilions, so that they appear embossed and gilded by its rays.

THE SOUTH FRONT (22)

The credit for the south front of the house, as with the whole of the South Vista, belongs to Earl Temple. As he inherited it in 1749, this was an amalgam of successive alterations and additions. In the 1740s Lord Cobham had filled in the spaces between the old house and the out-offices by adding suites of rooms on the first floor all along this side. They overlooked the garden but the long view of the front from the south was obscured by the narrow Abele Walk. Once this was cleared away and the full length of the house revealed (150 yards, twice the length of the north front), a new façade was essential.

Because of his advanced education in classical architecture, Lord Temple never put himself in the hands of a single professional architect. Equally, it has been suggested that such was his pride and tendency to meddle, none of the leading men of the

The Doric Arch frames a view of the Palladian Bridge, with Stowe Castle on the horizon in the distance; engraving by T. Medland

Robert Adam's design of 1770–1 provided the inspiration for the south front (Sir John Soane's Museum)

day would work for him for long. The design process seems to have taken 20 years by the time it was completed in 1774. It involved Borra, Georges François Blondel, Robert Adam and several of Lord Temple's relatives, including his brother-in-law William Pitt the Elder. According to James Dallaway, Temple's cousin Thomas Pitt 'was the sole designer of the superb mansion at Stowe', but this was overstating the case. Thomas Pitt was indeed the superintending architect and drew on his own design for the Corinthian Arch, but his starting point was Adam's design of 1770–1. This had involved a complex arrangement of four orders, admirable enough at close quarters but in the epic scale of the new South Vista, redundant. Pitt reduced everything to just two orders: 48 Ionic columns and pilasters extend along the whole length of the front and thread through the three groupings of 24 giant Corinthian columns and pilasters. Where Adam had drawn Venetian windows, Pitt's are of equal height, preserving the rhythm of the Ionic order. Seen from the terrace between the Lake Pavilions, the south front thus appears as the grandest of all Stowe's temples, and it sustains this grandeur even at a mile's distance when seen from Pitt's Corinthian Arch.

At the same time the central portico and loggia are magnificently detailed. All of the sculptural decoration was carried out by James Lovell: on the parapets of the side pavilions are his figures of Liberty and Religion (west), and Peace and Plenty (east); below them, in the lunettes, are medallions of Venus and Adonis flanked by scenes of sacrifice, and in the same positions to either side of the portico the

Four Seasons. Lovell also carved the gigantic Bacchic frieze (derived from the Choragic Monument of Lysicrates at Athens, published by Stuart and Revett in 1762). The ceiling and doorcase were derived from the Temple of the Sun, published in Dawkins and Wood's *Ruins of Palmyra* (1753).

THE DORIC ARCH (29)

The Doric, or Amelian, Arch was erected by Earl Temple in 1768 for three purposes: in anticipation of the visit of the Princess Amelia, George III's aunt, in July 1770; to provide a proper entrance to the Elysian Fields through the belt of trees bordering the South Vista; and to frame a view to the Palladian Bridge and beyond to Stowe Castle. Its architect was again Thomas Pitt. On 7 July 1770 Horace Walpole wrote to George Montagu:

The chief entertainment of the week, at least what was so to the Princess, is an arch which Lord Temple has erected to her honour in the most enchanting of all picturesque scenes. It is inscribed on one side *Ameliae Sophiae Aug.* and has a medallion of her on the other. It is placed on an eminence at the top of the Elysian fields, in a grove of orange trees. You come on it on a sudden, and are startled with delight on looking through it: you at once see through a glade the river winding at bottom; from which a thicket rises, arched over with trees, but opened, and discovering a hillock full of haycocks, beyond which in front is the Palladian bridge, and again over that, a larger hill crowned with the castle. It is a tall landscape, framed by the overbowering trees, and comprehending more beauties of light, shade and buildings, than any picture of Albano I ever saw.

A path which crossed the South Vista was aligned with the Doric Arch so that this view composed itself perfectly at the point bisected by the axis from the south portico to the Corinthian Arch.

On each side of the arch stood the statues of Apollo and the nine Muses that had been moved here after the formal parterres were levelled in the 1740s and the site renamed the Mount of Helicon (the home of the Muses in classical mythology).

THE OCTAGON LAKE

Rigaud's view of *The Great Bason, from the Entrance of the Great Walk to the House* (1733) shows a truly octagonal lake surrounded by a gravel walk, a scene created by Bridgeman in the 1710s and reminiscent of his basin in Kensington Gardens. It is scarcely recognisable in the present irregular sheet of water, whose edges were broken down by Earl Temple in the 1750s, but which is still known as the Octagon Lake. At its centre, according to an anonymous description of the gardens in 1738, was:

a Rustick Obelisk 60 feet high from the Water's Edge; it was originally designed to have formd a Jettau from the Top of it, and to have fell in a Continual Sheet of Water into the Bason below it, but for want of a due Supply of Water, this Intention cou'd not be put in Practice.

The obelisk fountain, or Guglio, was removed by Lord Temple when he was widening the South Vista in 1754.

THE LAKE PAVILIONS (20, 21)

Forming a backdrop to the Octagon Lake in Rigaud's drawing, these two 'heathen temples' are thought to have been designed by Vanbrugh in about 1719. They are not typical of his manner, but they were attributed to him as early as 1732. As he left them, they were simpler and closer together. They were pushed apart in 1764 by Earl Temple's great broadening of the South Vista, and at the same time 'modernised' by the addition of Neo-classical details devised by Borra.

Behind the eastern pavilion, built into the ha-ha, is an inhabited lodge serving the Bell Gate. This was the main public entrance to the gardens in the eighteenth and nineteenth centuries, and the point from which the guidebooks begin their descriptions.

THE ELYSIAN FIELDS

In his *Epistle to Burlington* (published in 1731) Alexander Pope urged all who aspired to emulate Stowe to 'Consult the Genius of the Place':

Start ev'n from difficulty, strike from chance;
Nature shall join you; time shall make it grow
A work to wonder at – perhaps a STOWE.

Nowhere was this formula put to greater effect than in Stowe's own Elysian Fields, which were being laid out in that year. This part of the garden, from the Grotto to the edge of the Octagon Lake, immediately became its most famous feature. Yet it was achieved only after years of difficulty.

Lord Cobham's early garden had been restricted to the west and south-west of the house by the route of the main road from Buckingham running north–south in the little valley to the east of the parterre. When around 1732 the old Roman road from Oxford was pressed into service as an alternative approach to the north front, Lord Cobham was emboldened to incorporate the valley in the garden.

Despite its name, suggesting the wide-open spaces actually to be found in the Home Park, the Elysian Fields is all in miniature, on an intimate scale. Partly in consequence of this, its buildings and planted effects had a far closer relationship with one another than those of the earlier garden. They also follow a more complex and carefully constructed plot. Notions of Elysium – the Paradise where heroes chosen by the Gods for immortality reside – abound in seventeenth- and eighteenth-century English poetry. To these, Lord Cobham and his literary friends and relations added a series of political messages that made Stowe the spiritual home of the 'Patriotic' opposition to the administration of Sir Robert Walpole (see p. 64).

The principal buildings here were all designed by William Kent, and it is probable that he had a hand in their landscape settings. In 1734 Sir Thomas Robinson wrote to the Earl of Carlisle:

There is a new taste in gardening just arisen, which has been practised with so much success at the Prince's garden in Town [ie Frederick, Prince of Wales's Carlton House] that a general alteration of some of the most remarkable gardens in the Kingdom is begun, after Mr Kent's notion of gardening, viz., to lay them out, and work without either level or line.... The

The Worthies River, with the Shell Bridge in the distance and the Temple of British Worthies on the right

celebrated gardens of Claremont, Chiswick and Stowe are now full of labourers, to modernise the expensive works finished in them, ever since every one's memory.

The former millstream was divided by the Shell Bridge into the Alder River (to the north) and the Worthies River below. Each had a quite different character: the Worthies River flowed between smooth lawns bordered by the 'lightest' of green foliage and bathed in sunshine (the true 'Elysian Fields'), while the Alder River had the more sombre character of the River Styx (which one must cross to reach the Elysian Fields), as Baron van Spaen van Biljoen described in 1791:

[The alder plantation] offers a deep retreat, wreathed in shade and impenetrable to even the brightest shaft of sunlight. Water laps at their roots, its very deep colour the result of the dark green of the chestnuts and alders which are reflected in it. The paths are covered in moss and lead to the Grotto of Contemplation. Pines and ancient gnarled elms, dead tree-trunks wreathed in ivy, the stillness of the water, everything in this deep solitude encourages meditation and inspires melancholy.

This mood had become all the stronger from the 1780s, when the Rococo decoration was abandoned in favour of the Picturesque taste.

The Elysian Fields are a landmark in two important respects: for working 'with the grain' of nature instead of imposing geometrical patterns on it, and as an experiment in 'moral gardening', a concert of landscape and architecture to induce a calculated series of moods and to transmit contemporary moral and political messages.

THE TEMPLE OF ANCIENT VIRTUE (30)

Although now largely obscured from the west, the Temple of Ancient Virtue, completed in 1737 to Kent's designs, was intended to close the long vista known as the Great Cross Walk which passed at a slight angle across the south front of the house (see the plan of 1739, p. 53). This arrangement followed Joseph Addison's vision of a 'great road' along which 'the middle-aged party of mankind ... marched behind the standard of Ambition' (see p. 5). The temple was raised on a grass mound, and its site was far more open than it is now. The design was based on the ancient Temple of Vesta at Tivoli, which Kent knew at first hand from his extended sojourn in Italy in the 1710s, and from Book IV of Palladio's *Quattro Libri*, here translated from the Corinthian to the Ionic order.

The temple is inscribed on the outside '*Priscae virtuti*' ('To Ancient Virtue') and was devised as a cenotaph to four Ancient Greeks who embodied the virtues that Lord Cobham found so lacking in the public figures of his own day: Socrates, Homer, Lycurgus and Epaminondas. The circular temple form has a solemnity and nobility well suited to memorial buildings, from Hawksmoor's great mausoleum at Castle Howard (1729) to John Russell Pope's Jefferson Memorial in Washington (1939). Bordered by laurel and elevated both by the grass mount and its own basement, with narrow stairs cut into it, this is an overtly *exclusive* building worthy only of a select few.

The four Ancient Greeks are represented by life-size Portland stone statues signed by Peter Scheemakers, and for which he was paid in 1737. These were sold in 1921, but have recently been replaced in the form of casts taken from the originals. The chosen individuals represent four of the five branches of public life referred to in Addison's essay – a general (Epaminondas), a legislator (Lycurgus), a poet (Homer) and a philosopher (Socrates). Above the niches are the following inscriptions (with translations taken from Defoe and Richardson's *Tour* of 1742):

I. EPAMINONDAS Cujus a virtute, prudentia, verecundia, Thebanorum respublica Libertatem simul & imperium, Disciplinam bellicam, civilem & domesticam, Accepit; Eoque amisso, perdidit.

From whose Valour, Prudence, and Moderation, the

The Temple of Ancient Virtue

Republick of *Thebes* received both Liberty and Empire, its military, civil, and domestick Discipline; and, with him, lost them.

II. LYCURGUS Qui summo cum consilio, inventis legibus, Omnemque contra corruptelam munitis optime, Pater patriae, Libertatem firmissimam, Et mores sanctissimos, Expulsa cum divitiis, avaritia, luxuria, libidine, In multa secula Civibus suis instituit.

Who having invented Laws with the greatest Wisdom, and most excellently fenced them against all Corruption, as a Father of his Country, instituted for his Countrymen the firmest Liberty, and the soundest Morality, which endured for many Ages, he having, together with Riches, banished Avarice, Luxury, and Lust.

III. SOCRATES Qui corruptissima in civitate innocens, Bonorum hortator, unici cultor DEI, Ab inutili otio, & vanis disputationibus, Ad officia vitae, & societatis commoda, Philosophiam avocavit, Hominum sapientissimus.

Who being innocent in a most corrupt State, an Encourager of the Good, a Worshipper of One only GOD, as the wisest of Men, reduced Philosophy from useless Indolence, and vain Disputations, to the Duties of Life, and the Advantages of Society.

IV. HOMERUS Qui poetarum princeps, idem & maximus, Virtutis praeco, & immortalitatis largitor, Divino carmine, Ad pulcre audendum, & patiendum fortiter, Omnibus notus gentibus, omnes incitat.

Who being the First of Poets, as he was the greatest, the Herald of Virtue, and Bestower of Immortality, known to all Nations, incites all, in a Divine Poem, honourably to dare, and resolutely to suffer.

The inscriptions placed above the doorways invite the visitor to reflect on the qualities represented by these four men, but also on their counterparts and opposites in modern life, as represented by neighbouring buildings on which the doorways were aligned:

Charum esse civem, bene de republica mereri, laudari, coli, diligi, gloriosum est: metui vero, & in odio esse, invidiosum, detestabile, imbecillum, caducum.

To be dear to our Country, to deserve well of the State, to be praised, honoured, and beloved, is glorious; but to be dreaded, and hated, is a matter of Ill-will, detestable, weak, ruinous.

Justitiam cole & pietatem, quae cum sit magna in parentibus & propinquis, tum in patria maxima est. Ea vita est in coelum, & in huc coetum eorum, qui jam vixerunt.

Maintain Justice, and thy relative Duty; which, as it is great, when exercised toward our Parents and Kindred, so is greatest towards our Country. That life is the Way of Heaven, and to this Assembly of those, who have already lived.

THE TEMPLE OF MODERN VIRTUE

Just to the south of the Temple of Ancient Virtue are the relics of the Temple of Modern Virtue, built at the same time to resemble the ruins of a classical building. And to contrast with the nobility of Scheemakers's four statues, there stood among the ruins a solitary mutilated torso in contemporary clothes. (George Clarke suggested that it might have represented Sir Robert Walpole, but so far there is no evidence of such a specific identification.) The significance of all this was well defined by an anonymous French visitor to Stowe in 1748:

The temple represents the flourishing state of Ancient Virtue, still untarnished and inviolate despite the passage of centuries; these tumbledown structures with their ruinous statuary are intended to show the fragility and the transience of Modern Virtue, decrepit even from the moment of birth. From which one can draw the following Moral: Fame founded on true virtue exists for ever, whereas Reputations built solely on popular acclamation evaporate as easily.

The contrast was heightened by the mowing regime: the grass of the bank and sloping lawn to the river was kept to four inches with the scythe, emphasising the perfect form of the Temple of Ancient Virtue, but left ragged and rough around the 'ruined' temple. Today's visitors may reflect on

The Temple of Modern Virtue in 1750; engraving from George Bickham's guidebook

the fact that after a further 250 years the Temple of Modern Virtue has almost completely disappeared among the roots of overgrown yew trees.

THE TEMPLE OF BRITISH WORTHIES (14)

It was Mercury who conducted the souls of chosen mortals across the River Styx to the Elysian Fields, and his marble bust (now gone) was placed in the oval niche set into the stepped pyramid which surmounts the Temple of British Worthies. This was adapted by Kent in 1734–5 from a design he prepared for the *exedra* in the garden at Chiswick of his great patron Lord Burlington, but which was not carried out there. At Chiswick, where it would have closed the main vista from the villa, or in Venus's Vale at Rousham (where Kent worked later in the decade), it would have sat more easily in the landscape, whereas at Stowe it seems at odds with the gradient. It had its origins in the Renaissance and Baroque gardens which Kent had studied in Italy,

such as that of the Villa Mattei at Rome (which has the same arrangement of steps), and the Villa Brenzone on Lake Garda, where busts of Roman emperors appear in a similar series of niches. But no emperor would have been eligible for inclusion in Lord Cobham's temple: this was a shrine to the Immortal Britons, and the most blatantly political of all his temples. The sixteen stone busts fall into two groups: on the left, those distinguished in the realm of Ideas, and on the right, those revered for their Actions, but they did not all assume their places from the start; for several years some of the niches remained vacant.

Of the sixteen, eight were carved by Rysbrack for the Temple of Fame overlooking the Home Park (now the Fane of Pastoral Poetry in Hawkwell Field) in about 1729–30 (Milton, Shakespeare, Locke, Newton, Bacon, Queen Elizabeth, William III and Hampden), and one, Inigo Jones, must have

(Right)   The Temple of British Worthies

Alexander Pope

Sir Thomas Gresham

Inigo Jones

John Milton

King Alfred

The Black Prince

Elizabeth I

William III

William Shakespeare

John Locke

Sir Isaac Newton

Sir Francis Bacon

Sir Walter Ralegh

Sir Francis Drake

John Hampden

Sir John Barnard

been supplied by him expressly for the Temple of British Worthies. The others were carved in about 1737 by Scheemakers. The inscriptions here are in English, so their implications could be readily understood without a guidebook in hand; variations in their length and quality show that they were also added progressively. In fact, it was not until 1763 that the last two, for Alexander Pope and Sir John Barnard, were added by Earl Temple, who was one of the collaborators in their composition. The others included some of Lord Cobham's many nephews, the 'Boy Patriots' or 'Cobham's Cubs' who regularly met in the Temple of Friendship: William Pitt the Elder, Lord Lyttelton and the poets Richard Glover and Gilbert West.

The poets, scientists and other artists of the left-hand arcade would have their place in any British Hall of Fame, but the political thrust of the temple is carried by the selection of 'Men of Action' to the right. These were all carved after Lord Cobham had resigned from official politics over Walpole's Excise Bill of 1733, and each of those selected can be seen to have had a modern counterpart. Thus King Alfred, who 'established juries, crush'd corruption, guarded liberty; and was the founder of the English constitution', was everything King George II was not, whereas Edward, the Black Prince, 'who preserv'd unalter'd … his natural gentleness and modesty', was identified with Frederick, Prince of Wales, who became the focus of the 'Patriot' opposition to George II and Walpole and who visited Stowe in 1737. Sir Walter Ralegh's inclusion symbolised the Patriots' denunciation of Walpole's Family Compact with Spain, concluded in 1733. Much of Lord Cobham's active life had been spent waging war in Europe, and he saw pacific measures such as the Family Compact as a surrender of all the gains of the Duke of Marlborough's generation, and fatal to Britain's trade. The inclusion of a modern merchant and MP for the City, Sir John Barnard (who was not only still alive but a staunch opponent of Walpole), among the Immortals pointedly implied the vicious, corrupt morality of Walpole himself.

A temple in a private garden may not seem the most effective medium for political opposition, but the message of the Temple of British Worthies received much wider currency when the inscriptions were published in full in the *London Magazine*

of July 1740, and again in the 1742 edition of Defoe's *Tour thro' the Whole Island of Great Britain*.

Several of the early visitors recorded a seventeenth 'Worthy' with the longest inscription by far, whose niche is in the back of the central block of the *exedra* and would have been viewed from the Thanet Walk:

To the Memory
of
Signor Fido
an Italian of good Extraction;
who came into England
not to bite us, like most of his Countrymen,
but to gain an honest Livelyhood.
He hunted not after Fame,
yet acquir'd it;
regardless of the Praise of his Friends,
but most sensible of their Love.
Tho' he liv'd amongst the Great,
he neither learnt nor flatter'd any Vice.
He was no Bigot,
Tho' he doubted none of the 39 Articles,
And, if to follow Nature,
and to respect the Laws of Society,
be Philosophy,
he was a perfect Philosopher;
a faithful Friend,
an agreeable Companion,
a loving Husband,
distinguish'd by a numerous Offspring,
all which he liv'd to see take good Courses.
In his old age he retir'd
to the House of a Clergyman in the Country,
where he finish'd his earthly Race,
and died an Honour and an Example to the whole
Species.
Reader,
this stone is guiltless of Flattery;
for he to whom it is inscrib'd
was not a Man
but a
Grey-Hound.

[THE MARQUESS OF BUCKINGHAM'S URN]

In a clearing in the shrubberies behind the Temple of British Worthies stood a large urn, inscribed in Latin and in English, and erected by the 1st Duke in 1814 in memory of his father. It was moved in 1931 to its present position within the school precincts.

THE SHELL BRIDGE (13)

The division of the Alder River from the Worthies River was achieved by means of planting and a dam, for which Kent designed this frontispiece or arcade not unlike the façade of his grotto at Claremont in Surrey. With its shelly decoration it was clearly intended to answer the Grotto further upstream. Early plans, from Sarah Bridgeman's 1739 publication onwards, show the ground between the bridge and the Alder River planted with trees and shrubs, or 'Forest Work', and eighteenth-century engravings confirm that it was intended to form a visual barrier between the two halves of the river. The bridge itself is not in fact the one shown in the engravings but a facsimile constructed in 1879, when the Duke of Buckingham's steward S. W. Savage reported to his employer: 'I have ... restored Shell Bridge according to an old drawing I has by me.' This was probably one of the engravings from Seeley's guides, but he may have been referring to a design by Kent that had survived in the Estate Office.

THE GROTTO (33)

At the Head of [the Serpentine River] is the Grotto, and on each Side two Pavillions, the one ornamented with Shells, as the other is with Pebbles and Flints broke to pieces. – The Grotto is furnished with a great Number of Looking-glasses both on the Walls and Cieling, all in artificial Frames of Plaister-work, set with Shells and broken Flints – a Marble Statue of *Venus* on a Pedestal stuck with the same.

Seeley's *Description* (1744)

On stylistic grounds, the Grotto is thought to have been designed originally by Kent in the 1730s. It was originally a rectangular temple built entirely above ground. With its 'looking glasses', statue of Venus (a copy of the *Crouching Venus* in the Uffizi at Florence), and what appear in Bickham's engraving to be long stools, it was far less of a grotto in the sense of a cave, than a sort of banqueting house. Its general plan seems thus to have resembled the Hermitage which Kent designed for Queen Caroline at Richmond *c*.1730. On either side were shell and pebble temples in a delicate rococo style. According to an anonymous visitor of 1738, the dome of the former was 'cover'd with the Shells of large Tortoises intermixed with small ones that close the Joints and Vacuitys'. The inside of the dome was decorated in quadrants with shells forming human faces. The same visitor conjectured that this most fragile of all garden buildings 'will prove too tender to resist the force of Winds and Weather', and in Seeley's albeit perfunctory engraving of 1763 the twisted columns are indicated as the stems of trees,

The Grotto in 1750; engraving from the Bickham guidebook

suggesting that these delightful buildings had melted into oblivion. They did so not long afterwards.

In 1780 the 1st Marquess of Buckingham decided to 'modernise' the Grotto by burying it. Connecting tunnels were built to give access from the sides, and earth from beneath and behind the buildings was mounded on top, which was then planted with the darkest of evergreens. In place of the more delicate earlier decorations, the Grotto now received encrustations of 'spars, fossils, petrifactions, and broken glass' and a marble tablet with lines from Milton, and the outside was covered 'with the roughest stones', according to Seeley, all to suit the new aesthetics of the Picturesque. The Grotto was now in harmony with its overgrown surroundings, a scene of pervading gloom that can be seen in Nattes's views of *c.*1805. The tunnels have recently been stabilised.

THE SEASONS FOUNTAIN (11)

Among the last additions to the garden, the Seasons Fountain is thought to be one of the monuments erected in honour of the visit of the Prince of Wales to Stowe in 1805. It is named after James Thomson's

The Seasons (1746), one of the most influential and universally popular poems of the eighteenth century, and inscribed with extracts from it. The fountain is unusual in being constructed in statuary marble, a material all too obviously unsuited to English gardens and to the iron-rich spring water it dispenses, and its origin as an eighteenth-century chimneypiece is not hard to discern (it is not known whether it came from Stowe or another house). Originally the façade of the fountain was decorated with Wedgwood plaques of the Four Seasons, and silver drinking cups were suspended on either side from chains.

CAPTAIN GRENVILLE'S COLUMN (32)

Capt. Thomas Grenville, RN, was one of Lord Cobham's nephews, the son of his sister and heir Hester Grenville and the brother of his eventual successor Richard Grenville, Earl Temple. In 1747 Capt. Grenville was fatally wounded while commanding the *Defiance* under Anson in the battle against the French off Cape Finisterre. He was buried in the church at Wotton, the Grenville family seat, and Lord Cobham raised this column in his memory at Stowe – the first embodiment of the

(Right) Captain Grenville's Column

The Seasons Fountain and Grotto in 1805; ink and wash drawing by J. C. Nattes

in judicio sisti; Columnam hanc rostratam Laudans & maerans posuit Cobham. Insigne virtutis, ehu! rarissimae Exemplum habes; Ex quo discas Quid virum praefectura militari ornatum Deceat M.DCC.XLVII

As a Monument to Testify his Applause and Grief Richard Lord Viscount Cobham Erected this naval Pillar to the Memory of his Nephew Captain GRENVILLE; Who, commanding a Ship of War in the British Fleet Under Admiral Anson, In an Engagement with the French, was mortally wounded in the Thigh by a Fragment of his shattered Ship. Dying, he cried out, 'How much more desirable it is thus to meet Death, than suspected of Cowardice to fear Justice!' May this noble instance of Virtue prove instructive to an abandoned Age, and teach Britons how to act In their Country's Cause!

In its new position, the statue of Neptune on top of the column was replaced in 1763 with John van Nost's lead figure of Heroic Poetry. This was one of the group of four types of poetry – Heroic, Pastoral, Satyric and Lyric – which came to Stowe in the 1760s, perhaps from Bubb Doddington's Eastbury House in Dorset. Facing towards the Temple of British Worthies, she holds a scroll which reads '*Non nisi grandia canto*' ('Of none but heroic deeds I sing'). Thus the Grenville 'cousinhood' elected one of their own to the realms of the Ancient and British Worthies.

CAPTAIN COOK'S MONUMENT (12)

Capt. James Cook's discoveries in the South Pacific in the 1770s encouraged Earl Temple to add a further monument in 1778 on the imperial theme already expounded by the Wolfe Obelisk and the Temple of Concord and Victory. Nattes's view of 1805 shows it surmounted by its great globe and positioned on the northerly island in the Alder River to which it was returned in 2003. It was moved to its present position in 1842. The plinth is inscribed '*Jacobo Cook/MDCCLXXVIII*' and inset with an antique marble profile of a man, pressed into service as an ideal likeness of Cook.

[THE GOSFIELD ALTAR]

'Duck Island', the southernmost island on the Alder River, was once the site of an Antique altar erected by the French King, Louis XVIII, in gratitude for

union of the two families that was to take place after his own death in 1749.

The Column initially stood to the north of the Temple of Concord and Victory. It is a rostral column (so called because of the ships' prows, or *rostra*, that protrude from its shaft), and originally supported a suitably heroic figure of Neptune flourishing a 'splinter of the ship', according to Lady Newdigate. Its designer is unknown, but since it is so closely based on antique sources, it may have been devised by Capt. Grenville's brother Richard (later Earl Temple).

In 1756 Earl Temple moved the column to its present position in the Elysian Fields, adding an inscription composed by his cousin Lord Lyttelton:

Sororis suae filio, THOMAE GRENVILLAE Qui navis praefectus regiae, Ducente classem Britannicam Georgio Anson, Dum contra Gallos fortissime pugnaret, Dilacerate navis ingenti fragmine Femore graviter percusso, Perire, dixit moribundus, omnino satius esse, Quam inertiae reum the hospitality his family had enjoyed at Gosfield Hall in Essex during their years in exile. It had been moved here from Gosfield by the 1st Duke in 1825. The altar disappeared from the island in 1842. Two rustic bridges once permitted closer inspection of this monument.

THE CHURCH OF ST MARY (31)

In removing the vicarage and the road to make way for the Elysian Fields, Lord Cobham spared the church, which was at least conveniently close to the house. It was, however, an encumbrance as far as the garden was concerned, and his intention seems always to have been to plant it out with a screen of trees and shrubs.

The core of the church dates from the late thirteenth century, with modifications and additions from c.1330 until 1975, when a memorial window by the Old Stoic Laurence Whistler was added in the south aisle. The east end was altered by the Marquess of Buckingham c.1790, and the two windows in the south aisle were carved in 1886 by Thomas Earp, who also worked on the Grenville church at Wotton.

The church remains in worship and does not belong to the National Trust. It is described in greater detail in Michael Bevington's *Stowe Church: A Guide* (1995).

[THE TEMPLE OF CONTEMPLATION]

Formerly on the site now occupied by the Seasons Fountain, and perhaps designed by Kent. Seeley's 1750 engraving shows a simple arcaded front below a pediment decorated with a profile roundel. Fairchild's plan, published by Seeley in 1763, shows its later use as a Cold Bath, drawing water from the spring that now feeds the Seasons Fountain.

[THE WITCH HOUSE]

Formerly in a clearing in the trees between the Temple of Ancient Virtue and the Mount of Helicon, it was built of brick with inwardly sloping walls and a heavy, oversailing roof. According to an anonymous 1738 description:

The Walls within are daub'd over with Scenes of an Old Witch and her Performances, drawn by a Dome-

stick of Lord Cobhams; but in such a manner, that though the Painter himself could make a Woman a Witch, he plainly proves himself to have been no conjuror. [The servant was one Thomas Ferrand.]

[THE GOTHIC CROSS]

One of the most ambitious productions of Eleanor Coade's Artificial Stone Manufactory, the Gothic Cross was erected in 1814 by the 2nd Marquess of Buckingham. It stood just to the south of the church amid the trees west of the Evergreen walk, of which it was the principal feature until the 1980s, when it was demolished by a falling elm. The newly reinstated walk was created by the 1st Duke as a meandering path fringed by yews, running from the Doric Arch to the Temple of Ancient Virtue. It is also planned to restore the base of the Gothic Cross on its old foundations, which can still be seen.

[THE 1ST DUCHESS'S URN]

Nearby stood a small white marble urn, now lost. It was erected by the 2nd Duke in memory of his mother.

The Gothic Cross in 1827; engraving from the Seeley guidebook

The Palladian Bridge with the tower of the Gothic Temple beyond

HAWKWELL HILL
AND FIELD

The enclosure of the land to the east of the Elysian Fields had begun in 1730–2, but it was not until the end of the decade that Lord Cobham continued the expansion of the garden into this area by breaking down the boundary that ran north–south along its eastern side and bringing the pasture known as the Hawkwell Field properly within the garden. This took the relationship of the garden with the surrounding countryside a stage further. In Bridgeman's time, it became possible to walk along the perimeter of the garden and to experience the wilds

of nature from the sanctuary of the ha-ha and parapet walls. Kent threw down the walls so that there remained no visual barrier between the garden and 'nature' beyond. In the Hawkwell Field nature was brought right into the heart of the garden, the sheep and cattle appearing within the garden itself to mingle with the buildings and to ornament the banks of the river. In literary terms, this was a progression from the notion of Elysium to that of Arcady, an ideal *earthly* pastoral paradise.

All the buildings in this part of the garden are by James Gibbs, who returned as Lord Cobham's architect at Stowe in 1739 after William Kent's period of favour in the 1730s. Here, at the eastern edge of the garden, Gibbs's buildings (which are all appreciably larger than those around the Home Park and the Elysian Fields) are disposed in the same spacious relationships that earlier characterised the Home Park. Although Whig politics played a part in the overall scheme, the associations are at one remove from the sharply contemporary political satire of the Elysian Fields, elevated from the vital issues of the day to a more generalised celebration of the true principles of Grand Whiggery.

THE GOTHIC TEMPLE (9)

The startlingly original triangular building presiding over the Hawkwell Field was designed by Gibbs in 1741. Although mentioned in Seeley's first guidebook in 1744, it was still not complete by 1748. Marchioness Grey, visiting that year, appreciated the siting of the building:

The Gothic Building half Church half Tower in Appearance, is the most Uncommon and best in its Way. It stands very high and expos'd, but in return makes a good Point of View, and has the finest Prospect over the Garden and Country of any.

The revived Gothic style was becoming familiar through publications in the 1740s, but in its essentials Gibbs's design was innovative in drawing so closely on actual medieval buildings such as Westminster Abbey and King's College Chapel at Cambridge.

The traceried upper windows of the temple were filled with 'curious Paintings upon Glass' (Seeley, 1748), apparently illustrating biblical subjects and heraldry, which according to Walpole were presented to Lord Cobham by Matthew Wise and removed from his house, Warwick Priory, but these do not survive. The internal walls were finished in the same way as the exterior but the ceiling of the central dome was by contrast encrusted with painted armorials referring to Lord Cobham's 'Saxon' forebears set on a gilded 'mosaic' background.

In 1756 Sanderson Miller, the quintessential amateur architect of 'Gothick', recorded in his diary that he was at Stowe 'contriving a finishing to Gibbs building', and Howard Colvin has suggested that this entailed the addition of the domed lanterns on the two lower corners, which do not appear in Gibbs's drawing.

(Right) The Pebble Alcove

(Left) James Gibbs's design for the Gothic Temple (Ashmolean Museum, Oxford)

(Right) The Gothi Temple in 1805; ink and wash drawing k J. C. Nattes

The Gothic Temple was dedicated 'To the Liberties of our Ancestors', but there are many features about it which would have suggested to contemporaries Lord Cobham's creed of Liberty without the need for prompting. The Gothic or 'Saxon' style (the terms were somewhat interchangeable) alluded to his supposed Saxon ancestors, the Earls of Mercia (see p. 57), and to King Alfred, whose putative foundation of the British Constitution and defeat of the Danes (celebrated in the inscription over his bust in the Temple of British Worthies) were taken as antecedents of the system of parliamentary democracy established in 1689 and the foreign policy of the Grenvillite administration of the 1750s. The very stone of which the temple is built, a particularly ferruginous Northamptonshire Sands ironstone, connoted Ancient Britain in contrast to the more polite, pale and immaculate stones of the various classical temples. Finally, the temple epitomised Liberty itself in appearing to stand so proudly amid the unkempt and untrammelled sward of the Hawkwell Field, and surrounded by free-growing trees.

There were, however, two more explicit emblems. Over the entrance Lord Cobham had in-scribed one half of a couplet from Corneille's play *Horace* (1639), in which Curiace declares: '*Je rends grace aux Dieux de n'estre pas Romain*' ('I thank the Gods that I am not a Roman'), so as to distinguish beyond any doubt British Liberty from Roman tyranny.

The temple is administered by the Landmark Trust, and there is no access to the interior.

THE PEBBLE ALCOVE (17)

Before the eastward extension of the Octagon Lake in 1827 and the removal of the Stone Bridge, this sheltered seat was originally more closely related to the Elysian Fields. It was built before 1739, probably to a design by Kent, whose Hermitage it somewhat resembles and balances on the opposite side of the South Vista.

Like the Congreve Monument, it was at its most effective when seen from the lake itself. Within, the alcove is decorated with pebbles in the form of Lord Cobham's coat of arms and his motto '*Templa Quam Dilecta*' ('How Beautiful are thy Temples'). The mosaics have twice been thoroughly restored, in 1877 and 1967.

LORD CHATHAM'S URN (10)

The large urn on the island on the north side of the Octagon Lake is known as the Chatham Urn. The original urn, now at Chevening in Kent, was carved by John Bacon in 1780 and was first erected at Burton Pynsent in Somerset by Hester Grenville, a sister of Earl Temple and the Countess of Chatham. It commemorated her husband, the famous states-man William Pitt, Earl of Chatham, who had died in 1778. The urn was given to the 1st Duke of Buck-ingham in 1831 and placed on the island with an inscription added by Lord Grenville. The original urn was sold in 1848, but, thanks to the generosity of the Trustees of the Chevening Estate, the National Trust has been permitted to make a copy to place on the island at Stowe.

CONGREVE'S MONUMENT (18)

The dramatist William Congreve (1690–1729) was, with Cobham and Vanbrugh, a member of the Kit-Cat Club, the fraternity of Whigs commemorated in Kneller's great series of 42 half-length portraits. In his poem 'Of Improving in the Present Time' (1728), Congreve addressed Cobham, his great friend and drinking-companion:

Sincerest Critic of my Prose or Rhyme,
Tell how thy pleasing Stowe employs thy Time.
Say, Cobham, what amuses thy Retreat,
Or Schemes of War, or Stratagems of State?
... Or dost thou give the Winds afar to blow
Each vexing Thought and Heart-devouring Woe,
And fix thy Mind alone on rural Scenes,
To turn the levelled Lawns to liquid Plains,
To raise the creeping Rills from humble Beds,
And force the latent Springs to lift their Heads,
On watery Columns Capitals to rear,
That mix their flowing Curls with upper Air?

Cobham's delightful monument to Congreve, orig-inally on an isthmus and from the 1820s on the island in a branch of the Octagon Lake, was designed by Kent in 1736. It is a stone pyramid applied with a well-rounded urn which bears a trophy of the dramatist's art. At the top sits an impudent monkey, a personification of the saying 'art is the ape of nature' and the quintessential Rococo animal, gazing at himself in a mirror. Beneath him are the inscriptions:

Congreve's Monument

Vitae imitatio Consuetudin[is] speculum Comoedia. Comedy is the Imitation of Life, and the Glass of Fash-ion.

Ingenio Acri, faceto, expolito, Moribusque Urbanis, candidis, facillimis, Gulielmi Congreve, Hoc Qualecunque desiderii sui [Sol]amen simul & Monumentum Posuit COBHAM 1736.

In the Year 1736, COBHAM erected this poor Con-solation of, as well as Monument of, his Loss of the piercing, elegant, polished Wit, and civilized, candid, most unaffected Manners, of WILLIAM CONGREVE.

THE TEMPLE OF FRIENDSHIP (16)

Despite its apparently universal dedication 'Amici-tiae S. —' ('Sacred to Friendship'), the temple was built for a small and particular group of friends. In 1737 Lord Cobham invited Frederick, Prince of

Wales to stay at Stowe. For those Whigs who went into Opposition after the Excise Crisis of 1733 (known as the 'Boy Patriots' or 'Cobham's Cubs' and consisting mainly of Lord Cobham's nephews), Prince Frederick came to embody the ideal of the 'Patriot King' in contrast to the rule of his father George II, and it was partly in commemoration of the visit that the Temple of Friendship was begun in 1739, the date inscribed on the outside with the dedication.

It was designed by James Gibbs as the first commission of his second period of employment at Stowe. Standing on the bastion created by Bridgeman at the eastern end of his southern terrace, it balanced Kent's Temple of Venus at the opposite end. The open arches to either side of the central block recall earlier belvederes at Stowe: Gibbs's Boycott Pavilions (see p. 11) and Temple of Fame

(later the Fane of Pastoral Poetry, p. 50), and the pavilions at either side of the Temple of Venus. Sarah Bridgeman's plan of 1739 shows how the avenues just south of the ha-ha admitted a view from the western belvedere of the Temple of Friendship to the Temple of Venus, and from the eastern side there was a view to Stowe Castle.

A more significant relationship was established in 1742–8 with the building of the Lady's Temple (later the Queen's Temple, p. 42), which Gibbs also designed and which faces the Temple of Friendship across the Hawkwell Field. This was to be the sanctuary of Lady Cobham and her friends, while her husband's political cronies resorted to the Temple of Friendship.

This temple is therefore unusual at Stowe in having had a regular use. It is built over a basement which had a kitchen as well, no doubt, as ample

The Temple of Friendship

cellarage. The central block originally had a low, pyramidal roof topped by an open lantern (see Bickham's engraving, illustrated below) and apparently covered with the same black glazed pantiles later used on the Temple of Concord and Victory. Within, it was decorated with murals by Francesco Sleter symbolic of Friendship, Justice and Liberty, as Seeley described in 1747:

Upon the Ceiling is seated *Britannia*: Labels, inscribed with the Reigns of *Edward 3.* and *Q. Elizabeth* are held on one Side of her; and on the other is offered the Reign of — [ie George II] which she covers with her Mantle, and seems unwilling to accept.

Around the walls were placed on tapering pedestals ten marble busts of members of Lord Cobham's political circle: Frederick, Prince of Wales, the Earls of Chesterfield, Bathurst, Marchmont, Chatham, Westmorland and Gower, Lord Lyttelton, together with Lord Cobham and Earl Temple themselves. The notches cut into the stone skirting to receive the bases of their black marble pedestals can still be seen. Scheemakers was paid in 1741 for three of the busts (Lord Cobham, Lord Chesterfield and the Prince of Wales) and Thomas Adye supplied that of Lord Westmorland. The authorship of the others is uncertain (all ten were sold in the 1848 sale).

Between 1772 and 1774 Earl Temple radically remodelled the roof of the temple. The lantern was removed and a high stone 'attic' added to the front; no doubt after 30 years' growth the surrounding trees had begun to obscure the building in the long view from the Queen's Temple.

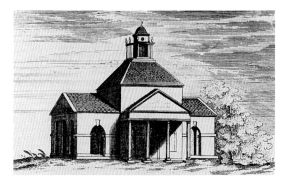

The Temple of Friendship in 1750; engraving from the Bickham guidebook

It was severely damaged by fire in about 1840, but retained as a ruin because of its prominence in several important views. Drawings by Edward Blore dated 1844 in the Stowe collection in the Huntington Library show proposals for rebuilding the temple as a Pantheon, but these were not pursued.

[THE IMPERIAL CLOSET]

Just to the east of the Temple of Friendship there briefly stood a tiny building known as the Imperial Closet, probably also built in 1739 to a design that Gibbs had published in *A Book of Architecture* in 1728. Its internal walls were painted by Sleter with full-length figures of the Roman emperors Titus, Trajan and Marcus Aurelius, respectively inscribed: '*Diem perdidi*' ('I have lost a day'), '*Pro me: si merear, in me*' ('For me, but if I deserve it, against me'), '*Ita regnes imperator, ut privatus regi te velis*' ('So govern, when an emperor, as, if a private person, you would desire to be governed'). The closet was dismantled by 1759.

THE PALLADIAN BRIDGE (15)

The Gravel Walk leads you from hence to a magnificent Bridge, now building, in order to make a Passage over the Serpentine River into the 3d Division of these New Gardens, which at present is no farther Executed than a Bare Design and choice of Ground for the Purpose. The Bridge consists of one large Arch, with a Smaller on each side of it; the Piers and Butments are Rustick from the Water's Edge to a Proper Height above the Crown of the Arches, and from thence the Work is carryd up with Windows, Balconies, etc. ornamented with Festoons, and other Peices of Carved Work and the whole is roof'd over from Side to Side, so that this Peice of Architecture not only carrys you over the Water, but if a Sudden Shower interrupts your Walk you here find a Shelter from the Water above you. A good Bridge that not only carrys one safe over, but also dry, under the Water.

Anon. MS, *Lord Cobhams Gardens 1738*

Stowe's Palladian Bridge was the second of three nearly identical bridges built in English gardens between 1737 and 1755. The first was put up at Wilton near Salisbury by the architect Roger Morris

The Palladian Bridge

in collaboration with his patron, Henry Herbert, 9th Earl of Pembroke, and the third at Prior Park on the edge of Bath for Ralph Allen, perhaps to the designs of Thomas Pitt. The Stowe bridge was probably built under the direction of Gibbs, and was completed in 1738, one year after the Wilton prototype. Although these bridges have always been called 'Palladian', they are not based on any known design by Andrea Palladio himself, and credit for their invention is more properly due to Roger Morris and the Earl of Pembroke. The

bridge at Stowe stood on the eastern boundary of Lord Cobham's garden, and because it was built as part of the carriage drive around the perimeter of the Hawkwell Field, it is the only one of the three without steps at either end.

It also sits lower in the water – an unfortunate consequence of damming the Octagon Lake to create a more picturesque effect. The addition of carved heads to the keystones of the three arches may have been intended to compensate for this loss of impact. However, the differences were originally far greater.

Whereas Lord Herbert's bridge was built as a

transparent, double colonnade, Lord Cobham's stood on the boundary of his land and was intended to block the view east of it. It had the character of a frontal loggia or balcony, with Scheemakers's relief carving of *The Four Quarters of the World bringing their Various Products to Britannia* occupying the space between the arched pavilions on the eastern side. Its scale and subject-matter must always have been at odds with the architecture, and it cannot have been properly visible either from within the bridge or outside it. To either side, in the arches, Sleter painted life-size standing figures of Sir Walter Ralegh holding a map of Virginia and William Penn with a book of the laws of Pennsylvania. Ralegh had already been enshrined among the British Worthies (see p. 29) and was an obvious companion for Scheemakers's sculpture. The specific inclusion of Virginia may have been a reference to Sir Walter's cousin Sir Richard Grenville (d. 1591), who was its first colonist, though not directly related to the Grenvilles of Wotton. The constitution Penn established for his colony was held up by the Opposition Whigs as a model of parliamentary government and toleration.

In May 1764 the mason Edward Batchelor was paid £17 for ten new columns and for enriching the architecture of the bridge following the removal of Scheemakers's relief. The relief was used to form the tympanum of the Temple of Concord (see p. 47). The 'enrichments' to the cornice and plaster ceiling were designed by Borra, on the pattern of those he had drawn at Palmyra for Dawkins and Wood's book of 1753.

A cascade was arranged at the end of the stream after the land to the east was bought by the 1st Duke of Buckingham in 1826.

[THE 1ST DUKE'S URN]

Until 1931, an inscribed stone urn stood by the side of the path that leads to the Lamport Gardens. Erected by the 2nd Duke in 1841, it commemorated his father, the 1st Duke, who laid out this portion of the gardens. It now stands in the Chapel Court of Stowe School.

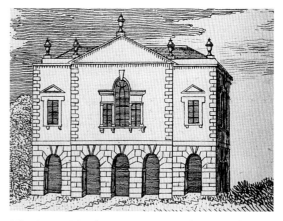

The Queen's Temple in 1750; engraving by G. Vandergucht from the Seeley guide

THE QUEEN'S TEMPLE (8)

Originally built as the feminine counterpart to the Temple of Friendship (see p. 38) at the opposite end of the Hawkwell Field circuit walk and called the 'Lady's Building', the Queen's Temple was probably designed by Gibbs around 1742 and completed about six years later. Its original form is shown in the early guidebooks (illustrated above); with a great room centred on a Palladian window over a rusticated basement with an open arcade in front, it must have resembled a small town hall. Inside the 'prospect room', Sleter painted murals describing feminine recreations, 'Ladies employing themselves in Needle and Shell-work' and 'diverting themselves with Painting and Musick' (Seeley guidebook, 1748).

Of Gibbs's building, probably only the basement survived the radical remodelling in 1772–4, when the great composite portico (based on that of the Temple of Diana at Nîmes) and steps were added to the south front and the first floor remodelled as a single space, probably to the designs of Earl Temple's cousin Thomas Pitt. Edward Batchelor's bill of August 1778 for 'Working and Laying the Circler Portico Ladys Temple' must refer to the addition of the charming bow on the north front, which may also have been designed by Thomas Pitt.

Yet further alterations were made in 1790 to commemorate the recovery of George III from madness after devoted nursing by Queen Charlotte, to whom the temple was rededicated. (The 1st Marquess's political position depended on the King's good health.) The changes were described in the 1797 edition of Seeley's guide:

The room is ornamented by Scaiola [scagliola] columns and pilasters, supporting a trunk-ceiling, taken from the design of the Temple of the Sun and Moon at Rome: At the West end is a Medallion of Britannia dejected, and with her spear reversed, and on the tablet the following inscription:

Desideriis icta fidelibus
Quaerit Patria Caesarem. [Horace, *Odes*, iv, 5, 15–16]
For Caesar's life, with anxious hopes and fears,
Britannia lifts to Heav'n a nation's tears.

On the East-end is a Medallion of Britannia with a palm, and sacrificing to Esculapius, on the recovery of the King from his illness; and on the tablet the following inscription:

O Sol pulcher! O laudande,
Canam recepto Caesare felix. [Horace, *Odes*, iv, 2, 46–8]
Oh happy day! with rapture Britons sing
The day when Hea'n restore their fav'rite King!

In the centre of this apartment is a magnificent setting figure of Britannia supporting a medallion of the Queen. — the figure is as large as life, and is placed upon a fluted pedestal, on which is the following inscription:

The Queen's Temple

Charlottae Sophiae Augustae, Pietate erga Regem, erga Rempublicam Virtute et constantia, In difficillimis temporibus spectatissimae, D.D.D. Georgius M. de Buckingham. MDCCLXXXIX
To the QUEEN, Most respectable in the most difficult moments, For her attachment and zeal for the public service, George, M[arquess] of BUCKINGHAM dedicates this monument. 1789.

On the walls of the centre compartment of this building are four medallions, representing 1. Trophies of Religion, Justice and Mercy. 2. Trophies of Agriculture and Manufacture. 3. Trophies of Navigation and Commerce. 4. Trophies of War.

Almost all of the sculptural decoration described by Seeley was executed in 1790 by Charles Peart, who had modelled the spectacular plaster triumphal procession in the frieze of the Marble Saloon in the house two years previously. The exception was the statue of Britannia, which is the only recorded work at Stowe by Joseph Ceracchi. In 1842 the 2nd Duke of Buckingham inserted in the centre of the floor a Roman mosaic pavement removed from the villa on his estate at nearby Foscott, which had been excavated in 1837–42.

The Queen's Temple became the home of Stowe School's Music Department. The columns of the portico weathered badly, and so in 1933–4 the School carried out repairs under the direction of Fielding Dodd and funded by an appeal. A further campaign of repair took place in 2003.

THE SAXON DEITIES (7)

The origin of Lord Cobham's commission to Rysbrack to carve seven Portland stone statues of the Saxon Gods who gave their names to the days of the week (*Sunna, Mona, Tiw, Woden, Thuner, Friga* and *Seatern*) lies in the long-standing belief in the Germanic roots of the English nation. More particularly, it was held that the Saxons brought liberal notions of government to Britain. This theory was expounded by Richard Verstegen in *A Restitution of Decayed Intelligence in Antiquities* (1605), in which the seven deities were illustrated by engravings that provided Rysbrack with the models for these statues. They were carved *c.*1727, and a few years later described in verse by Cobham's nephew Gilbert West, who made a genealogical connection between ancient and modern 'German' kings:

The Principal IDOLS of the SAXONS, *worshipd in* Britain.

The seven Saxon deities; an eighteenth-century copy of the illustration in Richard Verstegen's A Restitution of Decayed Intelligence in Antiquities *(1605)*

Tiw, ancient Monarch of remotest Fame,
Who led from Babel's Tow'rs the German Name.
And warlike Woden, fam'd for martial Deeds,
From whom great Brunswick's noble Line proceeds.

Stowe (1732)

Thus, Lord Cobham's commission could be called a celebration of the ideals of British Liberty embodied in the succession of Hanover.

Rysbrack's statues were originally set up in a circle around a seven-sided altar close to Nelson's Seat (see p. 37), a short distance to the west of the house. When the Gothic Temple was added in the 1740s, they were moved to accompany it on the eastern edge of the Hawkwell Field, but by 1773 they had once more migrated to a clearing in an oak wood nearer to the Queen's Temple which came to be known as the Wick (or 'Week') Quarter.

Rysbrack stood the deities on 'primitive' pedestals formed of massive blocks of stone, and their names were carved into their bases in an approximation of runic script. Each one was accompanied by a yew tree, which by 1905 had grown to cast a gloomy shade over the whole group. The statues were sold in 1921–2, but have all been located in recent years. The remains of their bases were discovered by archaeological investigations in 1992, and six of the seven have been replaced in replica.

Lamport Gardens

The land to the east of the Palladian Bridge and rising up towards the Gothic Temple belonged to the manor of Lamport, the property of the Dayrell family. When the 1st Duke of Buckingham purchased the estate in 1826, he demolished the old manor house. From 1840 the 2nd Duke, with his head gardener Mr Ferguson and the architect Edward Blore, laid out its surroundings as an ornamental rock and water garden. This was the last significant addition to the landscape of Stowe, and must have been Reptonian in character. Areas were set aside for particular effects: a fernery in a deep cutting, artificial rockwork, shrubberies and groups of moisture-loving plants and specimen trees. Gradually, exotic birds (including emus) and animals were introduced, and the whole area surrounded by a high wire fence to keep foxes out. The fence and the area within it are being restored by the National Trust.

THE CHINESE HOUSE (15a)

By its inclusion in the anonymous 1738 description of Stowe, this 'house built on piles, after the manner of the Chinese' may claim to be the earliest garden building in England designed in the Chinese style. It stood originally near the Elysian Fields 'in the middle of an old Pond', which is shown on Sarah Bridgeman's 1739 plan as a formal, coffin-shaped pool breaking the line of the ha-ha in an eastward direction from the Temple of Contemplation (see p. 34).

It was made of wood and painted on canvas both inside and out with *chinoiseries*, apparently by Francesco Sleter. Afloat on the pond were 'the Figures of two Chinese Birds about the Size of a Duck, which move with the Wind as if alive', and inside the building 'the figure of a Chinese lady, as if asleep' (Seeley). The Chinese House was moved to Wotton some time around 1750 and remained there for 200 years. It was recently acquired by the National Trust and because its original setting was so transformed by Lord Temple's improvements to the garden, it has been re-erected here, not in a pond, but on turf in the former Pheasantry. The restoration was carried out by public subscription as a memorial to Gervase Jackson-Stops, the Trust's former Architectural Adviser.

The Chinese House (after restoration)

THE GRECIAN VALLEY

The Grecian Valley is intended to complement and provide a setting for the Grecian Temple (now the Temple of Concord and Victory). This was to invoke a true sense of that Liberty which had its genesis in Greece and which now resides in Stowe's Temple of Liberty, the Gothic Temple.

The valley marks an end as well as a beginning in the history of the garden, and because Stowe can be seen as a paradigm of the eighteenth-century English landscape movement, of English gardens generally. It was the last great expansion of Lord Cobham's garden. Within 30 years his taste had moved from a preoccupation with regular arrangements of terraced lawns, statues and straight paths, from the disposition of plantings, buildings and ornaments to induce a calculated series of moods, or to illustrate poetic, political and satirical themes, to an essay in a three-dimensional landscape painting, the creation of an ideal landscape.

Lancelot Brown arrived at Stowe in March 1741 at the age of 25. Soon afterwards, there was a crisis of management in the garden, and Cobham lost two stewards in little over a year. In the autumn of 1742, he promoted Brown, who seems to have combined the roles of head gardener (with 30 men under him) and clerk of works, and to have had the direction of all that was going on in the garden, including building projects. Thus, in the course of laying out the Grecian Valley from 1747 to 1749, the first work in the style for which he is universally known, he was also supervising the raising of the Cobham Monument.

The character of the valley as a transition between the garden and the wider landscape to the north and east is aptly described by Thomas Whately in his *Observations on Modern Gardening*:

Lovely woods and groves hang all the way on the declivities; and the open space is broken by detached trees, which near the park are cautiously and sparingly introduced, lest the breadth should be contracted by them; but just as the valley sinks, they advance more boldly down the sides, stretch across or along the bottom, and cluster at times into groups and forms, which multiply the varieties of the larger plantations; these are sometimes close covers, and sometimes open groves; the trees rise in one upon high stems, and feather down to the bottom in another; and

The Grecian Valley
in 1805; ink and
wash drawing by
J. C. Nattes

between them are short openings into the park or the gardens.

Comparison of Sarah Bridgeman's plan of 1739 and Bickham's of 1753 shows the introduction of the Grecian Valley into what appears to have been tree-less pasture. That so much variety and subtlety of effect could have been described by Whately after only 30 years' growth may have been due to Brown's innovative use of a vehicle for transport-ing semi-mature trees from one part of the garden to another. In planting the sides of the valley, he probably made use of quite substantial trees removed from the south front. The creation of the valley also involved an earth-moving operation on a scale never before attempted here with spade, wheel-barrow and cart: in 1747 some 23,500 cubic yards of soil were moved by these methods.

In one important respect, Brown's plan for the Grecian Valley as a Vale of Tempe is incomplete. He attempted to create a sheet of water in the bottom of the valley as it turns into the Elysian Fields, but it seems the ground could not be made to hold it. However, the effect can be seen in seasons of persistently heavy rain, when this part of the valley temporarily floods. At the other end of the Grecian

Valley Lord Cobham planned a triumphal arch, but this was never started, and the view to the north-east was uninterrupted. It has subsequently been closed by later plantings.

[SCULPTURE]

Whately's French translator, M. Latapie, recorded the presence of 'several statuary groups in whitened lead ... the best of which are Hercules and Anteus [and] Cain & Abel, both pieces full of vigour.' These colossal lead groups were supplied by Andrew Carpenter in the 1730s. The *Hercules and Antaeus* is first recorded in another part of the garden in 1735; in 1756 Earl Temple decided to remove the Grenville Column to its present pos-ition close to the Temple of Ancient Virtue, and the *Hercules and Antaeus* took its place to the north-west of the Grecian Temple. The *Cain and Abel* (see p. 18) was part of the original iconographical scheme of the Temple of Venus and was moved to the far end of the Grecian Valley in 1765. These two groups, and a *Hercules and the Boar*, which also stood at the north-eastern end, all celebrate the triumph of physical strength, which would have supported the imperial programme of the valley when fully established in the 1760s. They were carefully positioned in the way that painters such as Claude used figures to frame a landscape and enhance the effects of perspective. Latapie's description provides useful evidence that such lead statues were frequently painted to resemble stone.

On a circuit of the valley towards the end of the eighteenth century, the visitor would also have come upon the antique figures of *The Athlete* and *The Dancing Faun*, also brought from other parts of the garden in the 1750s. The *Faun*, a copy of the famous *Medici Faun* in the Tribuna of the Uffizi, was positioned in a grassy glade in the centre of a circle of shepherds and shepherdesses, which were moved from around the statue of Queen Caroline in the Queen's Theatre in the early 1750s.

THE TEMPLE OF CONCORD
AND VICTORY (4)

The Temple of Concord and Victory at Stowe has been mentioned as one of the noblest objects that ever adorned a garden; but there is a moment when it appears in singular beauty; the setting sun shines on the long colonade which faces the west; all the lower parts of the building are darkened by the neighbouring wood; the pillars rise at different heights out of the obscurity; some of them are nearly overspread with it; some are chequered with a variety of tints; and the others are illuminated almost down to their bases. The light is gently softened off by the rotundity of the columns; but it spreads in broad gleams upon the wall within them; and pours full and without interruption

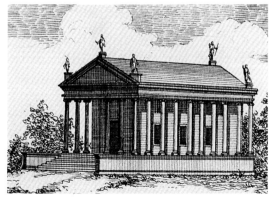

The Temple of Concord and Victory in 1750; engraving from the Seeley guidebook

on all the entablature, distinctly marking every dentil: on the statues which adorn the several points of the pediment, a deep shade is contrasted to splendor; the rays of the sun linger on the side of the temple long after the front is over-cast with the sober hue of evening; and they tip the upper branches of the trees, or glow in the openings between them, while the shadows lengthen across the Grecian valley.

Thomas Whately, *Observations on Modern Gardening* (1770)

The designer of the largest and by far the grandest of Stowe's temples remains unknown. The Grecian Temple, as it was first called, was begun in 1747 and roofed in 1749 within months of Lord Cobham's death at the age of 74. Seeley's 1788 guidebook ascribes the design to Kent, and goes on to say that the temple 'was designed from the measurements, which it nearly follows, of the Maison Carree at Nismes'. Kent died in 1748, and neither documentary evidence nor stylistic grounds support the attribution. There are resemblances between the temple and the Maison Carrée, a Roman temple of the late first century BC, but this is not only not 'Grecian' but also pseudoperipteral (having an engaged peristyle, whereas the columns surrounding the Temple of Concord are free-standing) and of the Corinthian order, and therefore built on a quite different system of proportion from the Ionic temple at Stowe. (For their recent restoration, see p. 86.)

In fact the Temple of Concord is not a copy of any known Greek or otherwise ancient temple, but rather a conflation of elements perhaps gathered from books available at the time, of which the Abbé Montfaucon's *L'Antiquité expliquée* (1722) and the Rev. Richard Pococke's *A Description of the East and Other Countries* (1745) are the most likely. The great series of publications which inspired the Neoclassical style in England – by Dawkins and Wood, and Stuart and Revett – were not published until the 1750s.

The Temple of Concord can thus best be called the first English building of Greek intention. It has been suggested that Lord Cobham's nephew and heir, Richard Grenville, later Earl Temple, may himself have designed it. In his portrait by William Hoare of Bath of 1760, he holds a plan of the Temple of Concord, and on his return from the Grand Tour in 1732 he may well have visited Nîmes. Two years later he was one of the founders of the Society of Dilettanti, which later promoted Stuart and Revett's publication.

The first recorded use of the term 'Grecian' at Stowe is a reference to the 'Grecian diagonal' in a bill in the garden accounts for 1747. This was the vista created from the Cobham Monument to the Grecian Temple, which must at that time have been under construction. There was no widespread fashion for 'Grecian' architecture at this time, but stylistic diversity is a notable characteristic of Lord Cobham's garden buildings. He had already built in the Palladian, Antique Roman, Gothic, Chinese and Egyptian styles, and it may simply be that he wanted to add what was thought to be the style of ancient Greece to the collection.

The temple underwent almost immediate modification in order to render it more truly 'Grecian'. A letter from Borra to Earl Temple dated 3 July 1752 marks his employment by Temple for the next two years to incorporate a *pronaos* (the vestibule formed at the eastern, entrance, end by the massive flanking inner walls), and to block the windows which had originally pierced the walls of the *cella* (principal space) of the temple and must

have seemed incongruous from the start. In 1755 six of the many lead figures supplied to Lord Cobham by Van Nost for his parterre some years earlier were raised to ornament the four corners of the roof and the two pediments. At the same time the black glazed pantiles with which the roof had first been covered were replaced with lakeland green slates.

In the late 1750s Earl Temple derived great satisfaction from the progress of the Seven Years War, not least because its political direction was largely conducted by members of his own extended family (see p.72). Between 1761, the year in which he resigned as Lord Privy Seal from the Pitt-Newcastle Ministry, and 1764, the Grecian Temple was once again in the hands of the builders, gradually assuming a new and powerful political significance and the dedication to Concord and Victory.

This process began in 1761 with the removal from the Palladian Bridge of Scheemakers's massive rectangular stone relief, *The Four Quarters of the World bringing their Various Products to Britannia*. In 1761–2 it was reassembled by the mason William Emberly as a triangle to fit the eastern pediment,

The Temple of Concord and Victory after the recent restoration of the pediment sculpture and flanking columns

with additional sculpture including that to fit the tapering corners supplied by William Stevenson.

The colossal stone figure of Victory bestowing a garland of laurel, which stands on the apex of the sculptural pediment, was probably carved by James Lovell, who carved the models for the plasterers employed on the temple. In this position it supplanted what was probably one of Van Nost's lead figures from the earlier garden, which is shown in the engraved views of the temple before its rededication. A number of different configurations of statues are shown on the roof in the many engravings and it is impossible from these or from other sources to tell whether a figure of Concord was added at the opposite end, or whether one of the lead figures persisted in that position. Lovell's statue has been reinstated and is accompanied by casts of the four original lead pediment figures, which are now at Anglesey Abbey in Cambridgeshire. The missing sixth figure was cast from a roughly contemporaneous statue at Castle Howard in Yorkshire.

Next, the blank walls of the *pronaos* and *cella* were furnished with a series of sixteen medallions, the majority of them based on subjects chosen by the Society of Arts for medals commemorating British victories. Most of these were designed by James 'Athenian' Stuart, and although as a member of the Society Earl Temple would have had known about this project, he is thought to have consulted Stuart directly in making this selection. Those on the walls of the *pronaos* were cast in terracotta by Lovell and represent *Concordia civium* (National Concord) and *Concordia foederatum* (Concord of the Allies: a British and a Prussian soldier hold between them a globe supporting a Victory). Over the door is an inscription from the Roman historian Valerius Maximus:

Quo Tempore Salus eorum in ultimas Augustias deducta nullum Ambitioni Locum relinquebat.
The Times with such alarming Dangers fraught,
Left not a Hope for any factious Thought.

Seeley's 1762 guidebook

In the nineteenth century the exterior of the temple was painted with an ochre limewash which unified the Helmdon and Ashendon stones of the columns and walls with the stucco of the brick walls to the *cella*; Scheemakers's Portland stone relief, and the pediment statues (variously Portland stone and lead) were also blended in by this method. The colour of the wash must have heightened the effect of the setting sun on the building described by Whately.

Within, the medallions were executed in terracotta and set into the walls within circular plaster frames 'suspended' from ribbon bows formed from strips of lead. The internal medallions are inscribed with lead lettering as follows (from the left of the door, clockwise), according to Seeley:

Quebec, Martinico &c., Louisbourg, Guadeloupe, &c., Montreal, Pondicherry, &c., naval victory off Belleisle, naval victory off Lagos, Crevelt and Minden, Felinghausen, Goree and Senegal, Crown Point, Niagara, and Fort du Quesne, Havannah and Manilla, Beau Sejour, Cherburgh, and Belleisle – executed from several of the Medals.

The ceiling was renewed in 1753–4 to a design by Borra based on those he had drawn for Dawkins and Wood's publication on the ruins of Palmyra. The interior was an entirely neutral, stone-coloured room, relieved only by the blue and gold colouring of the great doors, noticed by M. Latapie in 1771 and recently reinstated according to the results of cross-sectional analysis of the paintwork.

In the recent restoration, the Trust recreated the aedicule which completed the interior and formed the true focus of the building. Before it, on a low base, there stood from 1763 a figure of Public Liberty, in the place of honour reserved in classical temples for the deity, but this no longer survived at Stowe. Above the aedicule is an inscription from Valerius Maximus:

Candidis autem animis voluptatem praebuerint in conspicuo posita qua cuique magnifica merito contigerunt
A sweet Sensation touches ev'ry Breast
Of Candour's gen'rous Sentiment possest,
When public Services with Honour due,
Are gratefully mark'd out to public view.

Seeley's 1762 guide

A mutilated eighteenth-century draped torso discovered in a disused quarry on the newly acquired Home Farm Estate has been placed in the aedicule as a substitute for the missing figure of Public Liberty.

Seeley's 1763 guidebook mentions for the first time two further statuary marble groups, both of which had been supplied originally for the 1st Duke of Chandos's great house at Canons, near Edgware, in 1725. They were Scheemakers's *Venus and Apollo* and *Vertumnus and Pomona* by his partner Laurent Delvaux, and they stood in the *pronaos* to either side of the doors. By the time of Nattes's view of 1805 they had been replaced by two massive urns.

From the steps two oblique views complete the theme of political and imperial domination to the north, the soaring obelisk devoted to the memory of General Wolfe, military architect of the British victories over the French in Canada, and across the valley (via the Grecian Diagonal) the column celebrating one of its political architects, Lord Cobham.

The embellishment of the temple continued well into the nineteenth century. In the 1840s the 2nd Duke abolished the aedicule and its statue in favour of a new dais with a screen of granite columns. A plan to place bronze statues of Queen Victoria and Prince Albert on the dais to mark their visit in 1845 was abandoned in view of the Duke's debts; the royal couple each planted a pair of trees outside.

THE FANE OF PASTORAL POETRY (5)

In a glade in the wood at the far end of the Grecian Valley is the small open-sided temple or belvedere designed by Gibbs for Lord Cobham, and first set up as part of the early, western phase of the garden in September 1729. It was originally known simply as 'Gibbs's Building' and stood on a mound (accommodating an ice-house) in an almost exactly opposite relationship to the house, to the south-west, where it provided a viewpoint towards the Rotondo and the Queen's Theatre, and were surrounded by the series of busts by Rysbrack (Bacon, Hampden, Locke, Milton, Newton, Shakespeare, Queen Elizabeth and William III) which were later transferred to the Temple of British Worthies in the Elysian Fields.

Gibbs's Building was repositioned by Earl Temple in the 1760s to frame a view of Wolfe's Obelisk, which he had recently set up outside the gardens to the north, and was rechristened the Fane of Pastoral Poetry. The building also provided framed prospects over the surrounding park, reached via the shady groves of the Grecian Valley. Van Nost's lead figure of Thalia, the Muse of Pastoral Poetry, was placed just to the north of it. The statue was probably one of a tetralogy of poetry introduced in the 1760s. These statues were in addition to the existing nine Muses and Apollo around the Doric Arch. The four terms outside the Fane were copied from those now at Mottisfont Abbey (NT). The originals are at Port Lympne in Kent.

LORD COBHAM'S PILLAR (6)

Lady Cobham is building a model of the Trajan Pillar to the honour of her Lord, on the Top of which is to stand a statue of him.

Lady Newdigate's Journal, 1748

Fittingly, 'Lord Cobham's Pillar' is the tallest of Stowe's monuments (104 feet), and the one that can be seen from the furthest distances beyond the gardens. It was built during the last two years of his life, 1747–9, by which time all the main phases of the development of the garden were complete. Despite Lady Newdigate's observation, it bears only a passing resemblance to Trajan's Column in Rome, and there is in fact no classical precedent for its fluted octagonal shaft. It belongs to the period of Gibbs's second employment at Stowe, but if he provided an initial design, this was modified by Brown, who was in charge of its construction.

By means of a spiral staircase inside the column it was possible to see five counties from the little temple-belvedere, on which there stands a colossal statue of Lord Cobham in Roman armour. This was destroyed by lightning in 1957 and replaced in 2001.

In 1750 Brown observed, 'The Wind has a very great effect on Buildings that stand on so small a Base', and in 1792 four buttresses designed by Valdrè had to be added to the base. The walls between them were decorated with tablets inscribed with lines from Alexander Pope, and with a tribute to Lord Cobham. On each buttress was placed a rearing lion in Coade stone, for which Earl Temple paid £40 in 1778, and which by 1843 had been painted to resemble bronze. Three of them were also destroyed when the monument was struck by lightning in 1957, but were replaced with copies made by Christopher Hobbs.

The monument was built while the Grecian Valley was being laid out, and it is linked to both ends of the valley: to the north by Lord Cobham's Walk, and to Concord via the Grecian Diagonal. It also looks back to the Gothic Temple.

Lord Cobham's
Pillar

The Bourbon Tower in 1805; ink and wash drawing by J. C. Nattes

THE BOURBON TOWER (38)

In the deer-park nearby is a circular tower distinguished, like the Gothic Temple, from the other temples by the use of Northamptonshire Sands ironstone. Known at first as the Keeper's Lodge, it was built *c*.1741 by the same tradesmen that were employed on the Gothic building and was probably also designed by Gibbs. In 1808 it was renamed the Bourbon Tower to commemorate the visit of the exiled French royal family, who were living at Hartwell near Aylesbury. The tower's original conical roof was replaced in 1843, when the 2nd Duke employed Blore to turn it into a mock fort for the exercises of the Buckinghamshire Yeomanry, of which the Duke was commanding officer.

GENERAL WOLFE'S OBELISK (36)

To the north-west of the gardens, 'additions of Art' involved the moving in 1754 of the obelisk from the Octagon Lake to the middle of the fallow deer-park, where it was set up on a new plinth by William Smith and Richard Batchelor. Standing over 100 feet high, it was aligned on the Great Riding through Stowe Woods to the north, and back to the Temple of Concord and Victory to the south-east. Dedicated to General Wolfe, the victor of Quebec in 1759, it became the counterpoint to the Lord Cobham's Pillar, so that from the Temple of Concord and Victory one looked one way to a (late) political architect of victory over the French in the Seven Years War and the other way to one of the great military architects of that victory. James Wolfe had been a friend of the family and dined with Earl Temple the night before he sailed for Canada. The obelisk was restored in 2002.

THE CONDUIT HOUSE (35)

Near General Wolfe's Obelisk is a small octagonal pavilion known as the Conduit House. Dating from the mid-eighteenth century, it has the function of supplying water to the main house. It bears Coade-stone coats of arms dated 1793. Like General Wolfe's Obelisk, it was restored in 2002.

LAKES

Around the edge of the fallow deer-park, the upper reaches of the stream that passes beneath the Oxford Bridge were widened into another three lakes. First, the Roothouse River, a lake lying on the boundary between the Woody Park and Stowe Woods. Now locally called the Rufus River, it more probably takes its description from an agricultural building than a proper eighteenth-century root-house. (Stowe already had one in the gardens: St Augustine's Cave.) Secondly, the Haymanger Pond just above Dadford village, and thirdly, the

Home Farm Pond, which provided a head of water to run the sawmill and, in the nineteenth century, a turbine also. All these lakes were restored in 2002.

WOODY PARK AND STOWE WOODS

Beside the Roothouse River, and running across to the old main road to Towcester (called the Hog-back Lane), are the remains of the Woody Park. Brought into the deer-park in the latter part of the eighteenth century from Stowe Woods, it contained the deer barn and deer keeper's house.

Stowe Woods themselves were probably cut out of the medieval Whittlewood Forest in the six-teenth century, and by the time of Sarah Bridge-man's engraving in 1739, comprised a magnificent set of axial rides in the French manner, encouraging the eighteenth-century game of 'Spot the Steeple'. The Stowe Ridings were aligned on twelve churches and one windmill, and some were named as such: for instance, the Windmill Riding after Silverstone

The Conduit House

Windmill, and the Bow Brickhill Riding after Bow Brickhill church, 'the Pharos of Bucks', some 22 miles away. The main riding, the Silverstone Great Riding, was extended by the 1st Marquess of Buckingham in the 1800s as an avenue, and, after various intricate exchanges of land at Luffield Abbey (now the motor racing circuit), to Silverstone itself, where two further lodges were built on the main Northampton road. None of this part of Stowe belongs to the National Trust, but it can be accessed by public footpath.

NEW PARK AND COPPER BOTTOM LAKE

To the south of the gardens are the nineteenth-century red deer-park, interspersed with ordinary agricultural fields, albeit embellished with trees and avenues, and the greatest of the buildings outside the ha-ha, the Corinthian Arch.

The Buckingham River was widened through the New Park by the 1st Duke in the 1830s to take the outfall from the Eleven-Acre Lake at the southern end of the gardens. This seemingly simple task ran into problems when it was found that the subsoil was no longer clay or gravel (as with the upper lakes), but porous limestone, with the water table some twelve feet lower in the ground. Old stories that the lake had been lined with sheet copper (hence its local name of the Copper Bottom Lake) were partially verified in 1981, when the lake was relined in butyl sheeting, and many old copper rivets came to light in the silt.

SALES

The breaking-up of this landscape began in 1848 with the financial disasters of the 2nd Duke (see p. 80). During the 1850s his son, then the Marquess of Chandos, set in train sales of the estate to clear debts, which in 1845 totalled £1,464,959. Whilst trying to preserve the 10,000-acre core around Stowe and the family's other Buckinghamshire house at Wotton, he sold the estates in Ireland (8,900 acres), and other land and estates in Cornwall, Gloucestershire, Middlesex, Somerset, Oxfordshire and Northamptonshire, besides about 9,000 acres in Buckinghamshire itself.

These last areas were around Stowe itself and included all the land towards Water Stratford and Boycott (sold as the Boycott Estate), the land around Buckingham (sold as the Sackville Estate), and lastly Stowe Woods and Luffield Abbey to the north. These were bought by Lord Southampton, who was then building Whittlebury Lodge and putting together a 6,000-acre estate around it. Local stories relate that since the main road from Whittlebury to Buckingham was in such a poor state, he took to using the old Silverstone Drive past Stowe to get to Buckingham, until the 3rd Duke put a stop to this practice by blocking the Oxford Bridge.

The death of the 3rd Duke of Buckingham without male issue in 1889 led to further fragmentation, with Stowe itself and the greater part of the Estate going to his daughter, Lady Kinloss, and Stowe Castle and New Inn Farms to the Gore-Langton family, who inherited the Temple of Stowe earldom. The last of the Estate went in the final sales in 1921 and 1922.

RECOVERY

Since 1989 some of the more important parts of the designed landscape have been reunited with Stowe. In 1992 part of Stowe Castle Farm was purchased, thus preserving the first section of the Castle Riding (which originally ran from Stowe Castle to the north end of the Stowe Woods) to be replanted. Then in 1994 part of the New Inn Farm was purchased to protect the views from the lake around the Temple of Friendship and allowing the Bycell Riding to be replanted. At the end of 1995 the most important pieces, the Home Farm and the major part of the fallow deer-park, were bought with assistance from the Heritage Lottery Fund, enabling the restoration of General Wolfe's Obelisk, the Conduit House and the replanting of the north-east section of the Course (see p. 10), which in West's 1732 poem was represented as files of soldiers flanking the statue of George I, 'the Good Old King'. This acquisition also re-established the house and garden in its historic parkland setting.

CHAPTER FOUR
STOWE BEFORE VISCOUNT COBHAM

The Temple family of Stowe claimed descent from Leofric and his wife Lady Godiva, thus forming a link with the Saxon Earls of Mercia. The earliest evidence, however, locates them as yeoman sheep farmers near Witney in Oxfordshire. By 1546 Peter Temple was renting a sheep farm at Burton Dasset in Warwickshire, and in 1571 he took the lease of Stowe. The manor of Stowe had been confiscated at the Norman Conquest and given by King William to his half-brother, Bishop Odo. By 1149 it belonged to the abbey of Osney at Oxford and, eight years after the Dissolution of the Monasteries in 1539, it had become part of the endowment for the new bishopric of Oxford. Peter Temple was probably attracted by the suitability of the estate for sheep, but no less by the fact that the local town of Buckingham, one of the old rotten boroughs, had two MPs elected by only thirteen voters.

Peter's son, John, inherited Stowe in 1578 aged 36 and bought the manor eleven years later. He married a kinswoman of the Spencers of Althorp and was a JP and High Sheriff of Buckinghamshire. In thus establishing his family at Stowe he evidently deserved the description of 'frugal and provident'.

In contrast, John's son, Thomas, who inherited Stowe in 1603 aged about 37, was ambitious to the point of overreaching himself. He bought a knighthood on James I's accession in 1603 and then a baronetcy in 1611, as soon as the new order was created. Like his father, he was a lawyer of Lincoln's Inn, a JP and Sheriff of Oxfordshire (1606), Buckinghamshire (1616) and Warwickshire (1620); he was also an MP in 1588–9. His wife lived to see over 700 blood descendants, but the economic depression of the 1620s and his numerous surviving children led him into debt: his nine daughters needed marriage portions of £1,500 each, and his second son, John, cost some £16,000 to establish at Staunton Barry (now part of Milton Keynes). His eldest son, Peter, married Anne Throckmorton and thus acquired the Luffield estate north of Stowe. Already by 1625 Stowe Woods were laid out with ridings. Sir Thomas was forced to sell land, but despite an agreement with Peter he used the proceeds to add to the Burton Dassett estate. When he was sued for the money by Peter, he handed Stowe over to his son in 1630 and retired to live with a daughter in Warwickshire.

Sir Peter – he had bought a knighthood in 1609 aged 17 – established a large park at Stowe. One had

Sir Richard Temple, 3rd Bt, in a painting attributed to Henri Gascars (Stowe School). It dates from about 1673–8, when he was building the core of the present Stowe House and was about to lay out his Parlour Garden

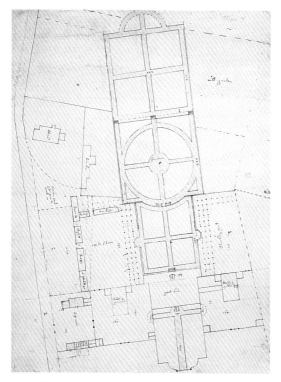

One of the schemes drafted around 1680, when Sir Richard Temple was planning his new Parlour Garden south of his new house and the avenues stretching down to the later Octagon Lake. Note the church to the east linked by the cross walk to the walled garden to the west (Huntington Library, San Marino, California)

existed in the early thirteenth century and in 1572 there was a small 'Old Park'. This was probably 'Owlde Parke' covering 77 acres, mentioned in the Abraham Allen's survey of 1633; it was doubtless the area known as Home Park by 1719. Sir Peter's first wife had died in 1619/20, and the year he took over Stowe he married secondly Christian Leveson, who brought with her a dowry of £3,000. He soon arranged for Allen's survey prior to enclosing the common fields in 1649. By then most of the villagers seem to have moved from the area around the parish church to the neighbouring hamlets of Dadford and Lamport. This allowed him to enclose a new park of 200 acres to the north-east of Stowe House, for which he purchased a herd of deer from Lord Spencer at nearby Wicken in 1651.

Sir Peter gained notoriety for quarrelling with his brother, suing his father and being openly rebuked in Parliament for maltreating his daughter. He was also an MP and High Sheriff in 1634, only to face severe difficulties in collecting Charles I's hated Ship Money tax. During the Civil War financial problems forced him to pawn his plate; thus he was in debt to 105 creditors for some £26,000 when he died in 1653.

Sir Richard succeeded as 3rd baronet aged nineteen, still a minor. He was rightly described as 'the fountain of exemplary contrivances', and, after most of his estates had been legally managed by his creditors for three years, succeeded in rectifying matters by mortgaging some of his properties to buy off over £19,000 worth of debts for £7,000. As MP for Buckingham he cultivated its thirteen voters assiduously, most famously in offering the timber for the rebuilding of the town hall in 1679. He was thereafter known as 'Sir Timber Temple'. Only in 1672 did he regain Westbury Woods. He was an MP for almost 40 years, becoming an expert on parliamentary precedent. During the 1660s he suffered from chronic indigestion. In 1672 he became Commissioner of the Customs with a handsome salary of £2,000. Three years later he married Mary Knapp, whose inheritance of £4,000 allowed him in 1676 to build a new mansion, still the core of today's house. Designed by William Cleare, it cost £2,600.

Just before the present house was built, Sir Richard had begun to improve his estate by planting a vineyard in 1668 and constructing a walled kitchen garden for apple and pear orchards near the present Menagerie in 1671–3. In about 1680, as soon as the new house was approaching completion, he began to plan the new 'Parlour Garden', stretching 200 yards south of the house, between the old Hey Way to the east and his recently built walled garden to the west. It thus replaced the 'oulde garden' west of the church, but allowed the retention of what were probably outbuildings from the old house, including the barn, stable, timber yard and hog houses. The series of sixteen proposals now in the Huntington Library show various schemes for dealing with the major problem: reconciling the alignment of the new house facing the steeple of Buckingham's original medieval church (blown down in 1699 and

The south front and Sir Richard Temple's Parlour Garden, probably as first constructed about 1683. This small formal garden was replaced by Bridgeman's parterres in 1717, which were in turn removed in 1742 to form the present sweeping lawn (Royal Commission on the Historical Monuments of England)

never fully rebuilt) with the north–south axis of the old house and the associated east–west Cross Lane. He laid out three levels of parterres or compart-ments as far as the Cross Lane. This stretched west-wards from the church and later became the Great Cross Walk; at first it doubtless allowed cattle to be driven from the old farmhouse to the hog pond and the later Home Park.

Around 1694 Celia Fiennes described the gardens as 'one below another with low breast walls and tareas [terrace] walkes ... replenished with all ye Curiosityes or Requisites for ornament, pleasure and use, beyond it are orchards and woods, with

rows of trees.' The Parlour Garden was planted with rows of cherry and apple trees in 1682, and in 1683 there were two fountains, one in a circular basin, as the gardener preferred, rather than oval, as Sir Richard wished, and one over seven feet high. It is just possible that two letters with advice from Sir Christopher Wren refer to the pipes and gates needed for this garden; William Cleare was his chief master-joiner.

Two other features completed the new grounds. South of the formal garden a narrow avenue of poplars was planted in 1682. This Abele Walk extended the vista towards the fish-ponds at the bottom of the valley where the Octagon Lake now lies. West of the walled garden, the wilderness was laid out in 1683. Its semicircular spread of paths was south of the site of the later Temple of Bacchus, stretching towards the Roman Road. For his last fifteen years Sir Richard seems to have enjoyed his new garden without making significant changes.

CHAPTER FIVE
VISCOUNT COBHAM

Sir Richard Temple, the 4th baronet, inherited Stowe in 1697, aged 21. He made his mark nationally as a general and a Whig politician. It is as the creator of Stowe's seminal garden that he is now best known, however, and this was partly the unforeseen fruit of time spent in the political wilderness. After Eton and Christ's College, Cambridge, he became an MP. He was made colonel of one of the three new regiments of foot raised in 1702, aged 26, and then served in Marlborough's campaigns. By 1710 he had been appointed lieutenant-general, one of five British officers of such a rank serving in Flanders.

During this time Sir Richard was also strengthening the family's dynastic ties. Two of his sisters, Christian and Hester, were married in 1708 and 1710 to Sir Thomas Lyttelton of Hagley and Richard Grenville of Wotton. Both matches were later important, not least because their descendants were included in the special remainder attached to Sir Richard's Viscountcy in 1718. In contrast, the line of his eldest sister, Maria, was excluded because she had married the Rev. Richard West, merely his regimental chaplain, against his wishes. In 1717 he bought out for £7,000 his second cousins William and Peter Temple, who would otherwise have inherited Stowe, if he had died childless.

His financial position improved rapidly. In addition to his army income and various sinecures, such as Constable of Windsor Castle from 1716, his marriage the previous year to Anne Halsey, a brewery heiress, brought in £20,000, while his lucrative venture at Vigo in 1719 enabled him to undertake further extensive work on his house and garden. His own social standing had also risen significantly. Although he was dismissed from the army by the Tories in October 1713, when Jonathan Swift called him 'the greatest Whig in the army', at the accession of King George I the following year he was rewarded by being raised to the peerage. He took the title of Baron Cobham from his grandmother's line, emphasising his own allegiance to the new Hanoverian monarchs by recalling the previous Lord Cobham's opposition to the first of the Stuarts. Four years later he was created Viscount Cobham and granted the special remainder. Thus, by 1719, when he was aged 44, he had the means and standing to make Stowe match his ambitions. Even by then he had faced and resolved so many problems; as James Craggs noted, he was a man 'who does not hate a difficulty', a theme echoed by Pope with regard to Cobham's gardening in his *Epistle to Burlington* (see p. 24).

Lord Cobham, painted around 1740, when he was 65, by Jean-Baptiste Van Loo (Stowe School)

A view of the parterre from the portico on the south front; engraving based on a drawing by Rigaud of 1733. The parterre was removed by Lord Cobham in 1742 as part of his naturalising process. Cobham sits in the left foreground, while his heir, Richard Temple, leans over his wife's shoulder

In the first decade after inheriting, Sir Richard was too busy to change much at Stowe. It was not until 1711 that he turned his attention to the garden and house. In October that year Lady Fermanagh recorded that 'he makes great improvements in ye gardens'. He began by reshaping his father's Parlour Garden south of the house, opening out the three small terraces into a vast formal parterre with a large basin and fountain; nearby he added the Sundial Parlour in 1717.

Even in 1713–14 the garden staff averaged only six men. His rapidly growing wealth, however, allowed Lord Cobham to increase numbers by 1718–19 to nearly 30, thereafter contracting out many of the tasks under foremen like John Gurnit, John Lee, William Nelson, Thomas Pease, Frank Rogers and William Turpin, some of whom are still recalled in the names of the walks they built. The

massive operations are evident from bills like the blacksmith's for the ironwork of 30 new wheelbarrows between October 1715 and the following March. Nothing could hinder the progress; even Edward Bissell, the head gardener from 1716, had to be carried around on a specially adapted chair after he broke his leg in October 1718. In July 1719 Vanbrugh wrote to Jacob Tonson that Lord Cobham was already spending 'all he has to spare' on improving his house and garden, something with which he was 'much entertain'd'.

After the south side, Lord Cobham turned to the northern approach. The Course was planted with avenues of elms in 1712, a canal was dug in 1716–18, and a mount where their two lines met was built in 1716–17. In 1718–19 he developed the triangle west of the house, towards Lee's Bastion on Nelson's Walk. He began with the heated greenhouse or orangery of two storeys in 1718 and the first garden buildings, such as the Temple of Bacchus and Nelson's Seat (both now gone). In 1719–20 he made his first hesitant moves into Home Park, refilling an early ha-ha when he decided to extend the garden even further. The Rotondo and the Queen's Theatre came next, allowing the garden to spread to the Octagon Lake and Lake Pavilions by 1722–3. This valley and lake provided a dramatic entrance for visitors at the bottom of the garden, a plan evident from 1717, when he built the New Inn on the old Buckingham road.

Lord Cobham's direct involvement in laying out the garden is always apparent: in 1714 he told his steward that he would 'be down in ten days and will then give directions about the step'. Nevertheless, to help realise his gardening ambitions, Lord Cobham called on Charles Bridgeman, the royal gardener, and his Kit-Cat friend Sir John Vanbrugh, the architect. The earliest record of Bridgeman's involvement is a bill for £1 2s 6d paid to 'Mr Bridgeman's man', probably from 1714. Later that decade a letter states that 'My Lord would not have it donn till Mr Bridgman comes'. By 1724 Lord Perceval noted that 'Bridgeman laid out the ground and plan'd the whole, which cannot fail of recommending him to business.' The garden now contained 28 acres and more than ten buildings, leading

Sir John Vanbrugh (1664–1726), Lord Cobham's Kit-Cat Club friend, who designed some ten garden buildings between 1719 and 1726. Portrait by Sir Godfrey Kneller (National Portrait Gallery)

Lord Perceval to add that Stowe had already gained 'the reputation of being the finest seat in England'. He was particularly impressed by the ha-ha. This allowed continuous vistas into the surrounding countryside without the unsightly and unnatural intervention of fences or walls. Its first recorded appearance at Stowe was as a 'stockade ditch' south of Lime Walk in February 1719, and it was used frequently thereafter by Bridgeman.

Vanbrugh's first recorded visit was in June 1719, but he may have helped Lord Cobham after being banished from Blenheim in 1716 following his arguments with the Duchess of Marlborough. His first garden buildings at Stowe, the 'little house' and 'sumer hous' (possibly Nelson's Seat and the Temple of Bacchus), date from 1719, and the Rotondo from 1720–1, and he also did much to enlarge the house. Vanbrugh obviously loved Stowe: in 1725 he spent two weeks there with his wife and Lord Carlisle of Castle Howard, telling

Charles Bridgeman (d.1738), the royal gardener, who laid out the original semi-formal garden between about 1714 and 1738. Portrait attributed to William Hogarth c.1725–1730, oil on canvas (Collection of the Vancouver Art Gallery, Founder's Fund, VAG 3409. Photo: Jim Gorman)

Tonson that Stowe was 'a Place now, so Agreeable, that I had much ado to leave it at all'. In March 1726 Vanbrugh died, so Lord Cobham then brought in another leading architect, James Gibbs, ignoring his Tory tendencies. That September Gibbs and Bridgeman were together at Stowe, and in May 1727 Gibbs was given 20 guineas. To the south-west about 60 acres were added to the garden, and Home Park was enclosed by a ha-ha providing a rural pastoral setting within the garden's terrace walks. The bottom of the valley was dammed to create the Eleven-Acre Lake. During his first period of employment in the 1720s, Gibbs added the Boycott Pavilions and the Temple of Fame (known as Gibbs's Building). Around 1730 Gibbs was supplanted by William Kent, one of the pioneers of the eighteenth-century landscape garden. Kent's Temple of Venus of 1731 was his first major contribution to the landscape at Stowe, and effectively completed the Western Garden.

Lord Cobham was not only famous for his military, political and gardening exploits, but also for his wide range of friends. He moved in a circle of wits and poets, such as William Congreve, a Kit-Cat Club friend like Vanbrugh. In 1728 Congreve praised Lord Cobham by addressing him in one of his poems:

Graceful in Form, and winning in Address
While well you think, what aptly you express,
With Health, with Honour, with a fair Estate,
A Table free, and elegantly neat.
What can be added more to mortal Bliss?
What can he want who stands possest of this?

Even better known as a poet was Alexander Pope, who is recorded as a frequent visitor to Stowe from September 1724. The following year he noted that he was 'still returning to Lord Cobham's [garden] with fresh satisfaction', visiting it and Wotton, and going again the next year with Swift and Gay. In 1731 he wrote his famous poem on the new style of gardening, choosing as his prime example Lord Cobham's work at Stowe. In a letter the same year he confided: 'If any thing under Paradise could set me beyond all Earthly Cogitations; Stowe might do it. It is much more beautiful than when I saw it before.' Following the death of his mother, it was Stowe to which Pope chose to retire. James

James Gibbs (1682–1754), who designed some nine buildings for Stowe between 1727 and 1741. Portrait by J. M. Williams (National Portrait Gallery)

Hammond, a minor poet who died at Stowe ten years later, wrote in 1732:

To Stowe's delightful scenes I now repair,
In Cobham's smile to lose the gloom of care.

Similarly another poet, Paul Whitehead, in 1738 again praised Lord Cobham's virtue and friendliness:

Ask ye, What's Honour? I'll the truth impart,
Know, honour then, is Honesty of Heart.
To the sweet scenes of social *Stow* repair,
And search the Master's breast – You'll find it there.

Such frequent comments on Lord Cobham's affability conflict with tales about his harsh nature. The tradition that he had the Silverstone poachers killed is probably a local exaggeration of their awful but less final punishment of transportation in 1736, while in 1741 his reprimand to his steward, William Roberts, 'a great favourite of Lord Cobham, ...

The Elysian Fields with the Temple of British Worthies. Although this drawing by Thomas Rowlandson dates from about 1805, Lord Cobham's original vision of a naturalised landscape bathed in light is still being enjoyed by picnicking visitors

vex'd him so much that he made away with himself.' The other side of Lord Cobham's character is seen in 1734, when Mr Berkeley recorded how 'two coachfuls of us' from Rousham had intended only to dine at Stowe, but had actually stayed three days, since 'it is enchanted ground, and not in people's power to leave when they please. Stowe is in great beauty, the master of it in good health and excellent spirits.' Indeed, on this occasion 'Pope diverted us by translating Horace'. Lord Cobham's generosity is evident in rebuilding part of Buckingham after the fire of 1725.

To allow the garden's extension eastwards, Lord Cobham rerouted the approach from Buckingham to the western side of the house in about 1732. This coincided with his retirement from politics to Stowe in 1733 for the second time, following the loss of his regiment because of his opposition to Walpole's excise scheme. Thus many of the temples in this part of the garden reflect in their iconography Cobham's dislike of Walpole and his love of freedom from corruption and tyranny (see p. 6). Here he enclosed 40 acres in the small but exquisite valley now known as the Elysian Fields, in which Kent constructed two of his best buildings, the Temple of British Worthies and the Temple of Ancient Virtue, linked by his Shell Bridge with the Grotto to the north. They are set in one of his earliest and most charming examples of naturalistic landscaping. In 1739 Pope wrote to Martha Blount: 'I never saw this Place in half the beauty & perfection it now has. ... This Garden is beyond description [in] the New part of it, I am every hour in it, but dinner & night, and every hour Envying myself the delight of it.' As Joseph Spence later commented, 'Lord Cobham began in the Bridgeman taste. 'tis the Elysian Fields that is the painting part of his gardens.'

Although in 1735 he reached the age of 60, Lord Cobham was fully abreast of the changes in gardening taste, if not leading them himself. Lord Perceval in 1724 had noted 'my Lords good taste' where, in Bridgeman's semi-formal plan, 'nothing is more irregular in the whole, nothing more regular in the parts'. Kent's new naturalistic approach of the 1730s heightened the tension between formalising 'art' and liberating 'nature', a contrast which must have appealed to Lord Cobham's enthusiasm for political liberty. Thus in 1736 James Thomson's *Liberty* included the lines:

See: Sylvan scenes, where art alone pretends
To dress her mistress and disclose her charms –
Such as a Pope in miniature has shown,
... And such as form a Richmond, Chiswick, Stowe.

By 1742 Samuel Boyse called his poem describing Stowe *The Triumphs of Nature* and began it by addressing 'Delightful Nature', but admitted that:

Here Art attends – and waits thy ruling will,
For she at best is but thy hand-maid still.

The year 1742 was, in fact, when Lord Cobham began to obliterate and naturalise the grand parterre which he himself had installed only 25 years before. Nevertheless others thought of Stowe as still primarily a formal garden dominated by classical buildings. Joseph Warton in *The Enthusiast or The Lover of Nature* (1744) wrote: 'Can Stow with all her attic fanes, such raptures raise As the thrush haunted copse?' In 1738 Bishop Herring admitted that at Stowe he would have 'beheld with contempt an artificial ruin', about the very time that Lord Cobham constructed the Artificial Ruins near the Octagon cascade. Similarly, the Marchioness Grey complained of Stowe that 'Nature has done very little for it, & Art so much that you cannot possibly be deceived.' Yet Stowe's natural charms could still please. Elizabeth Montague in 1744 wrote how 'Stowe ... is beyond description, it gives the best idea of Paradise that can be'.

The 1730s must have seen the height of Lord Cobham's entertaining at Stowe, especially once it had become his opposition power base after 1733. Here he trained his 'mob' of nephews, part of the 'patriot band' who eventually brought about Walpole's downfall in 1742. Since 1727, when his

William Kent (c.1685–1748), who designed some ten buildings for Stowe during the 1730s. Portrait by Bartholomew Dandridge (National Portrait Gallery)

brother-in-law Richard Grenville had died, the latter's son Richard and his four brothers and one sister, all aged sixteen or under, had been all but adopted by Lord Cobham. There were thirteen nephews in all, including Gilbert West, whose poem *Stowe* (1732) provided one of the earliest detailed descriptions of the garden. George Lyttelton and the younger Richard Grenville, later Earl Temple, both visited the classical sites of Italy. They then returned to support their uncle as MPs, and spent much time with him during the 1730s at Stowe; indeed many of the inscriptions were composed or selected by Lyttelton. The Temple of Friendship with its set of ten busts recalled the political alliances of 1739, and especially the visit two years earlier of the Prince of Wales along with Lords Chesterfield and Westmorland, all honoured with marble busts. Other visitors included William Pulteney, Lady Suffolk (Lyttelton composed an epigram for the bust planned for her at Stowe), Martha Blount, Hammond and, of course, Pope,

William Pitt (1708–78), the 'great commoner', was a frequent guest at Stowe and advised on its buildings. He married Lord Cobham's niece, Hester, in 1754. Portrait by William Hoare (National Portrait Gallery)

who in 1739 described a typical day: 'Everyone takes a different way, and wanders about till we meet at noon. At mornings we breakfast and dispute; after dinner, and at night, music and harmony; in the garden fishing; no politics and no cards, nor much reading.'

The most famous of the 'Boy Patriots', however, only became a nephew by marriage, and that after Lord Cobham's death. This was William Pitt, the Etonian contemporary of Richard Grenville and George Lyttelton. Lady Irwin described him as 'a very pretty speaker, one the Prince [of Wales] is partial to, and under the tuition of Lord Cobham'. Like Lord Cobham, he was deprived by Walpole of his army place and like the rest of the mob he spent much time at Stowe. The love-sick Hammond wrote in 1732:

There [at Stowe] Pit, in manner soft, in friendship warm,
With mild advice my listening grief shall charm.

In 1735 Pitt entered Parliament for Old Sarum, the rottenest of boroughs, but he spent the four months from July to October at Stowe. Here he amused himself with various games, noting: 'I was very stupid and play'd very well at cricket.' Another visitor and possible player was Lady Suffolk, who explained how 'I have learnt all the theory of cricket, and have some thoughts of practising this afternoon', despite her age of 47. No doubt she was an easy prey to the charm of flattery, since she recalled how 'Lord Cobham says I am the best-looking woman of *thirty* that he ever saw'. Pitt became so closely associated with Stowe that James Thomson, who spent much of 1734 and 1735 there, in his *Autumn* (1744) imagines enjoying his conversation above all others' at Stowe:

And there, O Pitt! thy country's early boast,
There let me sit beneath the sheltered slopes,
Or in that Temple where, in future times,
Thou well shall merit a distinguished name,
And, with thy converse blest, catch the last smiles
Of Autumn beaming o'er the yellow woods.

Not surprisingly, as Lord Cobham's cubs became more effective at worrying Walpole, so Lord Cobham's confidence in building a political satire grew too. The allegorical meaning of the painting on the Temple of Friendship's ceiling was far from difficult to understand, while the nearby Imperial Closet, the statue of *The Fighting Gladiator* and the Palladian Bridge all helped express his opposition to Walpole and his supporters. The Gothic Temple, or Temple of Liberty, crowning the Hawkwell Field in the Eastern Garden, was the culmination of his iconographical building.

Lord Cobham's sense of humour is apparent in his choice of a headless statue for the ruined Temple of Modern Virtue, sited carefully next to the resplendent Temple of Ancient Virtue. He was never very sympathetic to the established church, giving more prominence to a Witch's House and to Temples of Venus and Bacchus than to the old church of St Mary, which was concealed by planting. Although he employed able architects, his style was eclectic, mixing Saxon with Greek, Roman and Chinese for primarily political purposes; the Shell Rotondo, supposedly his only design and now gone, was equally individualistic.

In 1741 Lord Cobham was looking for a new gardener to succeed William Love. He wanted someone 'able to converse instructively on his favourite pursuit, but free from the vanity and conceit which had made his former assistants disinclined to alterations upon which he had determined.' His choice was Lancelot Brown, then aged 25. With Brown's help the last major area, another 60 acres, was added to the garden on its north-eastern corner. Slight hints of disagreements still persisted. Gibbs's published plan was changed before use at the Queen's Temple, and Brown's channelled flutes added to the Cobham Monument were 'not authorised by Gibbs', according to Earl Temple in 1765, while the Grecian Temple begun in 1747 had to be significantly rectified only five years later. Even the link between these buildings, the magnificent Grecian Valley, caused further problems. Although eager to finish 'the head of the oval', Brown assured Lord Cobham in 1746: 'I had

Lancelot 'Capability' Brown (1715–83), the head gardener at Stowe from 1741 to 1750. He was involved in laying out the Grecian Valley and constructing several buildings. Portrait by Nathaniel Dance-Holland (National Portrait Gallery)

never formed any other idea on it than what your Lordship gave me.' Indeed, visitors in 1748 reported several unexecuted plans for the floor of the valley, while in 1746 Anne Grenville referred to Stowe as 'the house of Discord'. It is just possible that Richard Grenville's radical views on the need to naturalise the garden were partly responsible. It was to his garden at Wotton that the Chinese House was taken in late 1748, when Lord Cobham removed it from its inappropriate site at Stowe. He had also countermanded his uncle's instructions to remove the plate from Stowe during the rebellion of 1745, and three years later he was responsible for building the Old Gaol in Buckingham after proposing a bill which Stanhope described as 'the arrantest job that was ever brought to Parliament'. Nevertheless, we have a picture of relative harmony from Hester, who recorded in 1748 that 'riding or walking is the amusement of the morning & Homer and cards of the evening'. A month later she reported that 'my Lord tells us every night it does not signifie to read unless we know how we apply what we read', and there was talk of a play to be enacted a few months later.

By the time of his death in 1749, Lord Cobham had established the present garden's framework and started its naturalisation. He had landscaped 205 acres, built over three dozen temples, laid out eight lakes or ponds, planted numerous avenues, built some four miles of ha-ha, had over 50 inscriptions carved, purchased over 40 busts and nearly 50 statues for the garden, and had the interiors of twelve garden buildings decorated with wall and ceiling paintings. His garden monument is the pillar supposedly erected to his honour by his wife in 1747–9, from which he could view his great achievement. The column is 104 feet high, and on top was his statue, suitably Roman in dress and, at 10ft 4in, much larger than life-size. Like Lucullus, he had proved himself a great general, grandee, gourmet and gardener.

CHAPTER SIX

EARL TEMPLE

Richard Grenville, later Earl Temple, succeeded his uncle at Stowe in 1749. He had long been groomed for the task and had developed his own ideas about gardening and architecture. Until 1770, however, he took an active part in politics, especially in conjunction with his brother, George Grenville, and his brother-in-law, William Pitt, Earl of Chatham, both of whom served as Prime Minister (1763–5 and 1766–7 respectively). In 1760 he became a Knight of the Garter, although he never achieved his proud ambition of a dukedom. In 1761 he resigned as Lord Privy Seal and four years later effectively withdrew from public life after refusing to become First Lord of the Treasury under his brother-in-law.

He married Anna Chamber, an heiress from Middlesex with £50,000, in 1737 at Lady Suffolk's Marble Hill House in Twickenham. Their only child died young and therefore he was likewise succeeded by his nephew, George's son, another George. On his mother's death in 1752, Richard

Grenville was described by his cousin Sir George Lyttelton as the richest subject in England. Much of this wealth he used to refine the garden and, from 1770, to give the house its present magnificent fronts.

From the first, Richard Grenville was eager to alter the garden. Following an amicable parting with 'Capability' Brown, he brought in a new gardener, Richard Woodward, from his old family seat at Wotton in 1750, although he did not technically inherit Stowe until two years later. He certainly had no qualms about making significant changes, since that very year he enraged his uncle's widow, now retired to Stoke Poges, by introducing sheep into the garden. Although this pastoral element was a logical result of creating an idealised Arcadian scene, Lady Cobham complained to Brown, whom she was employing at Stoke, that 'if my Lord Cobham cou'd know how Stow was used how vext he would be'. Grenville's sister Hester was also said to be 'in an uproar' over the sheep and later lamented the alterations to the form and

Chatelain's view engraved by Bickham of the Grecian Valley about 1751, soon after Richard Grenville had introduced the sheep so disliked by Lord Cobham's widow. The Grecian Temple (now the Temple of Concord and Victory) is to the right and the Grenville Column is in the foreground (it was later moved to near the church). The Queen's Temple is on the far left

shapes of her husband's 'dear paths' in the walks: 'Upon the whole their Beauty is Greater but their Merit less.'

His main emphasis at first was to naturalise the remaining formal areas of his uncle's garden. Thus, mainly from 1751 to 1753, he was concerned to soften the landscape. This was done by filling in the inward-facing ha-has of the Home Park and Hawkwell Field, removing the straight edges from the two old lakes of the Octagon and the Eleven-Acre, filling in the small formal canals on the North Lawn and east of the Rotondo, and reducing unnecessary avenues to clumps of specimen trees by felling along Gurnet's Walk and most of the Great Cross Walk.

The speed with which Earl Temple effected these naturalising changes is evident from Pococke's comment in May 1751: 'This place, now the trees are grown up appears much finer than it did formerly, and some alterations have been made by the present Lord in great taste.' In July Elizabeth Grenville, his sister-in-law, wrote that she liked 'most of the alterations extremely particularly the Queen Theatre & the Gothick feild' – the Queen's Theatre had lost its shepherds and shepherdesses.

It also seems that Earl Temple was ambitious to publicise the garden more widely. He therefore encouraged or allowed a free market in guidebooks (see p. 95). Earl Temple could not conceal his pride in his achievements at Stowe, asserting that they surpassed the best that nature could offer in Greece and Italy:

Tell me no more of Tempe's vale,
Nor boast of Arno's flowery dale,
Taste must confess, superior still,
The charms which decorate my Hill.

After the landscape had been mainly naturalised, Earl Temple was able to turn his attention to classicising the garden buildings. Although he may have started by altering the Artificial Ruins in 1751–8, the architect responsible for most of the changes during the 1750s was Giovanni Battista Borra. He was employed, from 1752, on modifying the Grecian Temple (now the Temple of Concord and Victory), perhaps because of his knowledge of the similar Graeco-Roman temple at Baalbec, which he

had visited the year before. Borra went on to modify the Rotondo in 1752–4, Gibbs's Building (now the Fane of Pastoral Poetry) in 1756, and the Boycott Pavilions in 1758–60. Earl Temple also had several smaller structures moved, such as Coucher's Obelisk (now gone) in about 1751, the Guglio in 1754, and the Grenville Column in 1756, along with many statues.

By the mid-1750s, therefore, now that he had restructured most of the landscape and a significant number of its buildings, Earl Temple naturally turned to the problem of rebuilding the house. By now the south front was an unattractive muddle of his uncle's ever larger additions. By 1753 Borra had supplied an impressive scheme for rebuilding, one that featured in many publications for several decades as actually constructed. In 1755, however, it seems that William Pitt pointed out some crucial difficulties in Borra's plan and Earl Temple applauded him: 'Where the Devil you picked up all this architectural skill, what Palladio you have studied I know not, but you are an Architect born & I am edifyed & delighted.' He added, about his brother James: 'So is Jemmy, that Goth, that visigoth, that antipodes of taste; He enters now fully into all the glorys of our future front.' In fact all that came of this initial attempt at the south front was the double flight of steps designed jointly by Borra and Earl Temple in the Servants' Hall in 1754.

It was therefore not surprising that his concern for the house and other matters let his enthusiasm for the garden wane a little. In October 1756 Elizabeth Grenville told Pitt: 'Lord Temple has once again caught the flame of gardening & says it now burns as bright as ever at which I think all his friends much rejoice from the great pleasure it affords him.' The extent of the further changes is evident from Hester Pitt's regrets as expressed to her husband: 'I cannot now follow your dear Paths in any of the Walks. Their Form and Shape is totally Alter'd.' The only exceptions which had been left unchanged were some of the earliest naturalised elements, such as the parterre and the buildings with some of the Grotto scenes. John Adam, brother of the more famous Robert, observed similarly in 1759: 'the formality and stiffness that formally prevailed in one quarter is now converted into more

Allan Ramsay's imposing portrait has captured well Earl Temple's sense of his own importance. It is dated 1762, when he was 51, soon after he had been awarded the Garter which he wears with such pride (Everard Studley Miller Bequest, 1965; National Gallery of Victoria, Melbourne)

natural and easy forms. Most of the hedges are taken away and the trees thinned in such a manner as to have a beautiful effect on the scenery.' He even complained of a defect, a swelling which has 'but one half in the garden and the other half left out', but admits that it is more likely to be an oversight than 'a scrimpedness or doing things by Halves', since the size of the garden and the number of buildings 'show forth a princely disregard for money'.

Earl Temple was soon back to his proud form, telling Hester in 1761: 'I am extravagantly in love – with Stowe; Sacharissa and amoret united! never, never was any thing half so fine and charming.' At about this time, after radically altering the garden

inside the ha-ha, he turned his attention to the wider landscape outside, especially the three approach drives, increasing their grandeur by abandoning naturalistic landscaping for the impressive formality of straight roads and avenues. In 1760 he built the Oxford Bridge and formed the Oxford Water, moving Kent's gate-piers to their present position. Further out he added a pair of Ionic lodges at Water Stratford, presumably laying out the straight road in-between. In the same year he built another pair of Ionic lodges at Luffield to mark the northern end of the Silverstone drive. All this must have meant sweeping away hedges and fences to improve the drives and enlarge the park, which by 1775 had grown to 585 acres. Finally, in about 1775, following the enclosure of Radclive-cum-Chackmore, he laid out the Grand or Stowe Avenue to the Corinthian Arch, perhaps his most impressive piece of landscaping. Thus Hester reported to William in 1761 what her brother had lately been doing, 'converting the Quality of the Ground, destroying Hedges, and making rivers &c.' From 1765 the drive through Culley's Park, linking the Corinthian Arch with the Oxford Entrance, enjoyed the magnificent reflection of the east Boycott Pavilion created by the Lower Oxford Water.

Inspired by these improvements, Earl Temple was able to return to altering and moving yet more of the garden buildings. A sudden burst of work in the first half of the 1760s included demolishing the Sleeping Parlour, further alterations to the Temple of Concord and Victory, rebuilding the back of the Palladian Bridge and the Temple of Contemplation, moving Queen Caroline's Statue, moving Gibbs's Building to become the Fane of Pastoral Poetry and moving the two Lake Pavilions. With the pressure of the impending royal visit by Princess Amelia in July 1764, in late June he wrote to Hester: 'Love & what is more, Money, will not procure me Masons to reedify fast enough my altered Fabricks. Why cant we move Buildings with as much ease as we do Pictures.' By now little in the garden remained as his uncle left it, as his cousin George Lyttelton observed the following year: 'the present Master of Stowe has taken off all the Stiffness of the Old Bridgeman Taste, and pulled down some of the Buildings, and altered others that were ugly very much the better; so the Place upon the Whole is vastly improved.'

He did not stop in 1764, however. The key to the next series of improvements was his decision in 1762 to fell the Abele Walk, the poplar avenue stretching from the former parterre down to the Octagon Lake; he called this 'the finest alteration I ever made'. This led in turn to moving the Lake Pavilions further apart in 1764 and building the Corinthian Arch on the horizon in 1765, to the designs of another Pitt, Earl Temple's cousin Thomas, then aged 28. The widened South Vista also forced him to implement plans for rebuilding the south front, now exposed from afar. But masterminding the details of numerous alterations was what appealed most to Earl Temple, as he told Hester in January 1769: 'We have passed our time here in the most perfect Solitude, & I can as truly say in the most perfect Content; all the Day with wheelbarrows, all the Evening with Accounts.' He worked hard and reported in 1762: 'I rise every morning a little after five and stick to business very handsomely. I dread the thought of confusion.'

Despite all his changes, Earl Temple's only new additions to the garden were a bridge, symbolically of wood (now gone), and the small Cook Monument, both in 1778, the year before his death. His plans for monuments to his brother-in-law William Pitt and his brother George Grenville were not executed. Cosmetic changes between 1772 and 1775 included work on the Queen's Temple, Nelson's Seat, Dido's Cave and the Rotondo.

Although he had vast wealth, Earl Temple was economical where possible. In 1750 he brought his Great Barn from Wotton to Stowe, and at Stowe he moved, rather than demolished, ten different buildings. Some parts were reused, such as elements from the Sleeping Parlour, while the balusters from the south front steps went to the Queen's Temple. Displaced statues from Lord Cobham's vast collection were redeployed around the Grecian Valley or on the Artificial Ruins.

His crude and brash sense of humour was not well received by many. It included spitting into Lord Hervey's hat during a reception at Stowe in 1750 – the outcome of a guinea's bet which he tried to pass off as a joke. His use of iconography was

Ramsay's portrait of Countess Temple contrasts clearly with that of the Earl. She was a poet, who despite her chronic ill-health, was devoted to her husband (Chevening House, Kent)

similarly idiosyncratic. He commemorated his political protégé, the radical John Wilkes, by giving the statue of Liberty on the South Front a squint like Wilkes's. Not surprisingly, his political scheming led him to be considered as the author of the polemical *Letters of Junius*. Horace Walpole, although happy to accept his hospitality at Stowe, called him 'this malignant man' who 'worked in the mines of successive factions for over thirty years together'. However, Temple's letters to his sister Hester, where he comes closest to opening his heart, show a more attractive side to his character.

Undisputed was his great pride and ambition, quite oblivious to others' sensibilities. Only fifteen days after his uncle died, he demanded that his mother, Lord Cobham's heiress, should be made a countess so that he could inherit her title. He then demanded the Garter and only acquired it in 1760 with Pitt's help; King George III was so angry that he supposedly threw him the ribbon with his head averted, as a bone is thrown to a dog. Unabashed, Earl Temple then immediately had his new honour featured in the house and on the entrance gateway for all to admire. He certainly was alone in regarding himself as Pitt's political equal; no doubt he intended the Temple of Concord and Victory to be as much a celebration of their political union as of Pitt's victories in the Seven Years War. Ironically, his obstinate pride led to a serious rift with Pitt from 1765 to 1769, despite Hester's efforts to reconcile the two. It was this quarrel which broke Pitt's health in 1767 and sent him into retirement. As Harold Spender remarked in 1924 of this quarrel: 'The Grenvilles lost us America; but I verily believe that they thought England sufficiently compensated by gaining Stowe.' Even the intended cenotaph to William Pitt at Stowe was probably to include his own statue. He hoped for a dukedom, but in this he was disappointed.

Earl Temple continued his uncle's custom of using the garden to entertain his numerous visitors. Just as the Grotto had been illuminated during the summer of 1744 soon after its construction, it began to form a regular venue for candle-lit suppers with accompanying music. Princess Amelia, King George III's aunt, twice experienced such outdoor amusements during the climatic vagaries of an English summer. At 10.30pm on Friday, 17 July 1764, near the end of her five days at Stowe, Her Royal Highness walked down to the Grotto using the new flight of steps on the south front which Earl Temple and Horace Walpole found so difficult because of their gout. The garden was illuminated with 1,000 lights and filled with over 1,000 spectators. In front of the Grotto an illuminated ship provided a picturesque platform for the musicians and the Alder River was covered with floating lights; 20 gallons of oil were burnt in two hours. 'Nothing was seen but lights and people. Nothing was felt but joy and happiness,' ran one optimistic report. After her cold supper the Princess returned before midnight. Since it had been raining for the previous three days, it must have been a cold and damp affair. Lord Coventry remarked that 'the Stowe party ended badly, the weather bad, – the wine bad – and the ceremony intolerable.'

On Thursday, 5 July 1770, Princess Amelia again braved supper in the Grotto. This time the cold was so intense that Horace Walpole, 'having some apprehension of the consequence, desired when we came back a glass of Cherry Brandy by way of prevention.' At least it was not raining, since after dinner and before the supper that evening they took coffee at the Doric Arch (named Princess Amelia's Arch), where Horace Walpole had carefully arranged that a piece of paper with his poem to the Princess should be discovered in the hand of Apollo's statue nearby. The next day the Princess was taken fishing on the Eleven-Acre Lake, although others were embarrassed that she did not succeed in achieving the highest catch.

Other visitors followed their own interests. The Gothick architect Sanderson Miller, who was at Stowe eight times in 1750, once for a whole week, walked in the garden with the company and 'Capability' Brown for five hours in November 1749. One morning, perhaps in 1756, he spent indoors 'with Mr Pitt and Lord Temple, contriving a finishing to Gibbs building [the Gothic Temple]', and had 'conversation … with Mr Pitt and Lord Poulteney etc about happiness', spending the evening 'singing at the Grecian Temple'.

The death in 1770 of his brother George Grenville, the former Prime Minister, led to Earl Temple's last and greatest sequence of work at Stowe. This was the rebuilding of both grand fronts of the house. He was now aged 59 and increasingly lived in retirement from politics at Stowe. Earl Temple's heir was George's eldest son, also George, now in his guardianship, and that year George offered Earl Temple for rebuilding the south front the considerable income which his father had obtained for him from a government sinecure in 1764 when he was only twelve years old. The offer spurred Earl Temple into renewed action, although it was several more years before Thomas Pitt's alterations to Robert Adam's plans produced the magnificent façade that we see today, said by Lord Nuneham to surpass 'in majesty and beauty everything I have seen'.

Earl Temple was fully in command throughout. He rejected the advice he had sought from William and Thomas Pitt about the location of gateways on the north front screen walls, and the projecting

The magnificent south front of the house, Earl Temple's last and greatest building project. It took eight years' work from 1771 to just before his death in 1779. The 2nd Duke commissioned this drawing by Joseph Nash to commemorate Queen Victoria's visit in 1845; she can be seen near the top of the lawn (Royal Collection)

portico on the south front was said to be his own idea. He was equally ready to criticise Robert Adam's imprecise use of classical details. Not surprisingly, 'the Plans for the Garden Front', as he told Hester in 1770, 'at present ingross most of our Time & Conversation.' He even had the foundations for the south front taken up the next year, apparently to allow for the projection of the south portico. That Earl Temple should have chosen Pitt's graceful simplification of Adam's fussy and unclassical details is a tribute to his now refined taste and judgement.

The effort took its toll, however. In 1772 he confessed to 'many and many disappointments', and the next year Hester wrote that he was 'in no Spirits, and having a bad opinion of Himself'. Two years later he told her: 'I have more than once agreed, when vexed in spirit, with wise King Solomon, that all is Vanity and Vexation.' The following year his wife wanted to abandon Stowe for Eastbury in Dorset, another of their houses, but her husband preferred to soldier on amid the building works. Indeed, despite his serious illness early in 1775, he was still 'wheeled among his workmen', but he had to talk to his steward out of his nurse's

sight. Although 'every symptom marked approaching death', he was supposedly saved by 'quantities of wine, & the strongest cordials'. By 1776 Lady Temple was not surprisingly 'low spirited', and on her death the following year her husband was 'much dejected, more so even then I expected', according to his nephew. Nevertheless he again rallied to the great challenge and later that year wrote to William Pitt: 'This same Hill of Stowe, on which we have spent our Happiest days perhaps, though not your most glorious, is so changed, that you would scarce know it again.' Even in his last hours, in September 1779, 'his deliberations turned solely upon his buildings'. He had in fact, after almost nine years, outlived the completion of the south front by just five months. 'Long Legs' or 'Squire Gawky', now a lonely widower isolated in an unfinished palace amid a vast garden and park, met his end after being 'thrown out of a chaise on a heap of bricks' while driving at Stowe.

CHAPTER SEVEN

THE 1ST MARQUESS AND 1ST DUKE OF BUCKINGHAM AND CHANDOS

Under the Marquess of Buckingham, Earl Temple's nephew and successor, Stowe reached the height of its splendour. George Grenville had many advantages. His early stammer was corrected by Sheridan and he went on to possess 'a fine selection of language'. His father was Prime Minister and on his death in 1770, his uncle at Stowe became his guardian. In 1774 he undertook the Grand Tour and the next year married Mary Nugent, an Irish Catholic heiress aged sixteen and supposedly with £14,000 per annum. In 1779, aged 26, he inherited Stowe, but he was busy elsewhere for most of the first ten years.

In politics he did not achieve his greatest ambitions. Although he was twice Lord Lieutenant of Ireland (1782–3, 1787–9), and was created Marquess of Buckingham in 1784, he had hoped for a dukedom. He therefore resigned as Secretary of State after only three days in protest. In contrast, his cousin, William Pitt the Younger, became Prime Minister in 1783 aged 24, and was succeeded in 1806 by his youngest brother, William. The third brother, Thomas, was an ambassador and bibliophile. Their income was vast, much of it public money: William Cobbett reckoned that the three brothers received some £900,000 from the state. But their income shrank when they lost office, and even the rent rolls of a substantial estate could not support the Marquess's ambitious plans for Stowe.

The Marquess's biggest changes were to the grand approaches. Before 1797 he realigned the end of the main drive at an angle to the house, thus demolishing Nelson's Seat, and moved the statue of King George I to its present position. He spent much on enlarging the estate, planting the Oxford Avenue in 1804, but shortage of money probably made him abandon the plan to continue it in a direct line to Tingewick. Near the Corinthian Arch he added the two milliary columns, and at the south-

ern end of the Grand Avenue he built the Barracks in 1802 and the two Buckingham Lodges in about 1805.

Within the garden the Marquess mainly restricted himself to repairs and embellishments, no doubt partly for financial reasons, since by 1804 money was said to be running short. He reused a chimney-piece, perhaps from the house, for the Seasons Fountain, by 1805. With Valdrè's help, he strengthened the Cobham Monument in 1792 and re-decorated the Queen's Temple in 1790. Below the south front he installed the stone balustrade in 1790 with its pair of flower gardens. In 1792–4 he repaired Stowe church and introduced classical ceilings inside the house. As a solace after his wife's death in 1812, the Marquess enlarged the garden, enclosing 28 acres of the park east of Lord Cobham's Pillar. He also finished his uncle's steady clearance of buildings, such as the Pebble Rotondo, St Augustine's Cave and the visible remains of the Pyramid. By now he must have agreed with Thomas Jefferson, who in 1786 called the garden the 'pleasure grounds', regarding Stowe primarily as a place of entertainment. He had the Menagerie built c.1781 for his wife as a refuge from the crowds of visitors in the house, doubtless employing Valdrè to decorate the central circular room. The Marchioness naturalised the appearance of Dido's Cave and partially buried the Grotto. In the back of the Orangery she founded a village school.

As with his uncle, politics remained important. In March 1789 the Marquess was still in Ireland, a position which depended on George III remaining

(Right) Sir Joshua Reynolds's portrait of the 1st Marquess and Marchioness of Buckingham with their young son, later the 1st Duke. Lady Buckingham was a skilled musician and artist – she studied under Reynolds – and had an impish sense of humour (National Gallery of Ireland, Dublin)

Richard, Earl Temple, later 1st Duke of Buckingham and Chandos, by Sir William Beechey, c.1802, when he was 26 (Stowe School)

return than the interest charged. When he shut up Stowe to save costs in 1827, he spent two years on his yacht touring the Mediterranean collecting antiquities. He was reputedly the heaviest man ever to be carried up Mount Vesuvius. His Italian purchases comprised eighteen crates of statuary and a further 30 large packages containing works of art. His personal expenditure was also out of control: in October 1820 he had bought 84 hats for £180.

The dukedom was not the family's only ambition. They had also long coveted the neighbouring Lamport estate which the 1st Duke eventually purchased in 1826. He was thus the last of the family to extend the garden, enclosing seventeen acres on the south-eastern corner. He then enlarged the Octagon Lake, and the head gardener James Brown added a small cascade below a picturesque rock and water garden east of the Palladian Bridge. In 1831 the garden designer J. C. Loudon thought that the garden had been greatly improved since 1806 by Brown, 'who may justly be said to have received

domination of national politics for the previous half-century.

The 1st Duke added greatly to the collections in Stowe House through his marriage in 1796 at the age of twenty to Anna Eliza Brydges, then aged only sixteen; the marriage had been arranged ten years before in Bath. As the heiress of the last Duke of Chandos, she brought considerable wealth and the Chandos name. The dispersal of many great continental collections following the French Revolution provided further scope for the Duke's acquisitiveness. He was one of the buyers at the Orléans sales in 1798, and while he continued to buy paintings for the next twenty years, he also amassed large collections of engravings and books, commissioned a lavish porcelain service and indulged his scientific and archaeological interests on a massive scale.

Extravagance came naturally to him, and he made few economies until they were forced upon him with the sales that started in 1833. He still borrowed money to buy land yielding a lower

Anna Eliza, Countess Temple, later Duchess of Buckingham and Chandos, by Beechey, c.1802. Her son, later the 2nd Duke, is at her side (Stowe School)

Festivities in the snow outside the north front at the coming-of-age of Earl Temple, later the 2nd Duke, in February 1818

the mantle of his great namesake and predecessor in the same garden'. The 1st Duke made some minor changes. In 1814, within a year of inheriting Stowe, he erected the Gothic Cross, perhaps in memory of his mother, and added the Evergreen Walk, an inscription to his mother at Dido's Cave and an urn in memory of his father. Like his father, he was reluctant to remove many buildings, despite repeated criticism of the excessive number, such as Prince Pückler-Muskau's in 1818: 'It is so over-crowded with temples of all kinds that the greatest improvement that could be carried out here would consist in pulling down about ten or twelve of them.'

In the 1820s he turned part of the Menagerie into a museum and laid out the Upper and Lower Flower Gardens with a new fountain nearby. As his portly physique indicated, he valued his kitchen gardens highly and had brought in Brown to superintend them, only later putting him in charge of the pleasure grounds. Despite his growing financial problems, he insisted on repairing the Temple of Venus in 1827–8. He also demanded rhododendrons in the Alder Valley and, in 1831, a new American border. That year, however, Loudon reported that the

garden was not kept as before, 'the number of hands being yearly lessened. In new and rare plants, trees, and shrubs, the grounds are not keeping pace with the nurseries.'

The 1st Duke was probably responsible for the new deer-park to the south-west of the garden. This formed a picturesque setting for his new Queen's Drive and its two New Ponds of *c*.1821. The old park to the north was thus freed for cavalry drill practice and a cannon range. He also extended the private carriage drive to Silverstone, building the present pair of stone lodges where it joins the main road. He also probably erected the Chackmore Fountain beside the Grand Avenue in 1831 (demolished in the late 1950s).

There were relatively few jamborees at Stowe during the 1st Duke's time, partly because of his growing financial troubles and partly because his wife preferred to live at Avington in Hampshire. Nevertheless on a snowy February day in 1818 his son's 21st birthday was celebrated in the now customary way, with thatched booths and an ox roast on the north lawn. Again, true to his extravagant nature, the 'Stowe Junket' at his grandson's baptism in June 1824 may have been the largest ever: over 190 guests stayed in the house alone and many more were lodged in Buckingham for the week, while a ball for 1,100 was held in an ordnance tent sent by the Duke of Wellington.

CHAPTER EIGHT
DECLINE AND FALL

Richard Plantagenet Temple-Nugent-Brydges-Chandos-Grenville, 2nd Duke of Buckingham, took the royal element of his name from his mother's family. With a personal income of £14,000, he could have afforded to live in reasonable state, but he inherited and developed the 1st Duke's extravagant tastes and talent for embezzlement, and displayed a fatal plausibility that made many of his friends easy victims. He went to Oxford but did not take a degree and instead entered politics, becoming the leader of the landed Conservatives in the House of Commons from 1816. He sponsored the Chandos Clause added to the Reform Bill in 1832 and resigned as Lord Privy Seal in 1842, earning the title of 'The Farmers' Friend'.

Expense was no object. After Wotton was burnt in 1820, it was rebuilt by Sir John Soane. His main joy, as Jackson's portrait (illustrated on this page) implies, was the Buckinghamshire Yeomanry. He probably replaced the dark blue and gold of Stowe's old livery, still the School's colours, with the Grenville green of the new yeomanry uniforms, for which he paid. At his son's baptism in 1824, his great-aunt complained that he was much more concerned with his yeomanry than his heir; in fact the following year he gave away the gilt christening cup to a private for winning a horse race in the park. Fittingly, his monument at Stowe is the obelisk erected by his yeomanry in the old Drill Park near the Bourbon Tower.

Once he inherited Stowe in 1839, the 2nd Duke sold a thousand pictures, but this was merely to make room for further acquisitions. He also succeeded in deceiving his creditors long enough to undertake a vast programme of repairs to the house and garden buildings during his first five years. With Edward Blore as architect, he re-sited many of the smaller monuments and statues. He was particularly fond of stone urns and vases, erecting monuments to

The Marquess of Chandos, later the 2nd Duke, painted by John Jackson in 1829 (Stowe School). He is wearing his Grenville green Hussar uniform as commander of the Buckinghamshire Yeomanry, which he supported financially to prevent its disbandment by the government in 1829

Queen Victoria arriving at the north front in January 1845.
On parade were 500 labourers dressed in white smocks and
a contingent of the Yeomanry

both his parents and the Queen of Hanover. He also spent vast sums on rebuilding much of the kitchen garden in Dadford. To strengthen security, he constructed Garden, Lamport and Water Stratford Lodges, and employed several army pensioners as gatekeepers. He had little understanding of landscape gardening and erected fences and walls where he fancied, enclosing his father's picturesque Lamport or Japanese Gardens with a wire fence, to keep the foxes away from his pheasants and exotic birds. His greatest joy must have been turning the Bourbon Tower into a mock fort and creating the cannon and rifle range close by.

Although the 2nd Duke was keen to deter unwanted visitors, he was equally anxious to attract royalty to Stowe. Thus in January 1840 there was a visit by the Duke of Cambridge, an uncle of Queen Victoria, and his son, Prince George. In August that year William IV's widow, the Dowager Queen Adelaide, visited, together with the Archbishop of Canterbury. Disraeli understood that 'the outdoor part, as far as triumphal arches, processions, crowds

in the gardens, &c, was very successful.' The King of Hanover and the Duchess of Gloucester came in 1843. The following year the Duke laid on a grand gala for his son's coming-of-age, but this was aimed at persuading him to sign over his destined inheritance to his spendthrift father.

The climax came in January 1845 when his friend, the Prime Minister, Robert Peel, persuaded Queen Victoria and Prince Albert to stay at Stowe. The Duke was already in debt to the staggering sum of over £1 million, but he borrowed yet more to cram his house with new furniture. The pair of oak and cedar trees outside the Temple of Concord and Victory is the only obvious reminder of this visit. He hoped to turn the Temple's interior into a commemorative shrine, but his impending ruin prevented its completion.

In August 1847 the Duke's effects were seized by bailiffs acting for a cartel of his creditors, and he fled abroad. His affairs were taken over by trustees in consultation with his son, the 24-year-old Marquess of Chandos, who was suddenly aware that his father had for several years been making fraudulent attempts on his inheritance.

In March 1848 most of the outlying parts of the estate, in Ireland, Hampshire and London, were sold, but the market was soon flooded and most of it went very cheaply. Likewise, the great sale of the contents by Christie's, which lasted for 40 days from 15 August to 7 October 1848, raised only £75,400. Writing in *The Times* on 14 August, Macaulay lamented:

During the past week the British public has been admitted to a spectacle of a painfully interesting and gravely historical import. One of the most splendid abodes of our almost regal aristocracy has thrown open its portals to an endless succession of visitors, who from morning to night have flowed in an uninterrupted stream from room to room, and floor to floor – not to enjoy the hospitality of the lord, or to congratulate him on his countless treasures of art, but to see an ancient family ruined, their place marked for destruction, and its contents scattered to the four winds of Heaven. We are only saying what is notorious ... that the Most Noble and Puissant Prince, his Grace the Duke of Buckingham and Chandos, is at this moment an absolutely ruined and destitute man. ... Stowe is no more.

What now seems most remarkable about the catastrophic events of 1848 is that they did not in fact mark the end of the family at Stowe. By 1861, when the 2nd Duke died in the Great Western Hotel at Paddington ('from the splendour of a prince to the grade of a lodger'), his son Richard had recovered the family's affairs sufficiently to return to live at Stowe. In 1865 Disraeli could write that 'the flag waves once again over Stowe, which no one expected'.

Since 1847 the future 3rd Duke and his agent Thomas Beards had executed a policy of retrenchment over the whole estate, while still preserving its Buckinghamshire core of 10,000 acres. The house was mothballed, the garden staff reduced from 40 to four and much of the garden left for grazing, while the garden buildings received minimal maintenance. From 1848 onwards, not just the outlying woods, but all but one of the great avenues was sold for timber.

From the 1860s the accounts show expenditure on new furnishings for the house, and on repairs to the garden buildings. The Palladian Bridge was overhauled, the Temple of Friendship consolidated, and the Bell Gate refurbished and reopened to admit visitors to the gardens. The garden staff was restored to some 30 men, and new plantings undertaken, in particular cedars along Pegg's Terrace on the southern edge of the garden, and sequoias on the Paddock Course Walk to the north of the Grecian Valley. The Upper and Lower Flower Gardens established by the 1st Marquess were also restored. The Museum by the Lower Flower Garden was restocked with fresh curiosities, such as 'a fine specimen of the sacred bull of the Hindoos', a granite sculpture excavated by the Duke while serving as Governor of Madras from 1874 to 1880.

The 3rd Duke's achievement in rescuing Stowe was in its way as great as the work of those who created it, but he could never entirely recover the status of the family. On his death in 1889 he left no male heir, despite having married for the second time four years previously, and the dukedom became extinct after only 67 years. Stowe passed to his eldest daughter, Mary, Lady Morgan-Grenville, who also inherited the title Lady Kinloss, but she had no use for the house and considered selling.

The widowed Lady Kinloss returned for a short while to Stowe in 1901 after a brief and bizarre interlude of five years in which it had served as the court of the Comte de Paris, exiled claimant to the French crown, who had previously been accommodated at Claremont and Whittlebury.

In 1908 the coming-of-age of Richard, Master of Kinloss, grandson of the 3rd Duke and heir to Stowe, was marked with celebrations that recalled the great fêtes of the early nineteenth century, with 400 tenants seated for lunch. But the resemblance was entirely superficial.

The Master of Kinloss was killed in the first few months of the Great War. When peace returned, his younger brother put the Stowe estate on the market, and it was sold with some of the contents and garden statuary in July 1921 to Mr Harry Shaw of Beenham Court, near Newbury, for £50,000. Most of the remaining contents and statuary were sold on in the following year.

(Right) The Palladian Bridge was repaired by the 3rd Duke in the 1860s

CHAPTER NINE
RECOVERY

Our immediate and worst forebodings regarding Stowe have been most happily dispelled by the generous intervention of Mr Shaw of Beenham Court. . . . Certainly there are few places better worth while preserving or better suited for public delight and education. Properly arranged and wisely administered Stowe might become a great cultural centre.

Clough Williams-Ellis, *The Spectator*, 23 July 1921

As a result of this article, Clough Williams-Ellis found himself appointed as architect to the governing body of Stowe School, which purchased the house and garden from Mr Shaw in October 1922. His first work was in adapting the main body of the house to form classrooms and dormitories; the school received its first pupils in May 1923.

The quality of the buildings and landscape were central to the educational ideals of Stowe's first headmaster, J. F. Roxburgh, who was appointed at the age of 35 and very swiftly established its reputation: 'If we do not fail in our purpose,' he wrote, 'every boy who goes out from Stowe will know beauty when he sees it all the rest of his life.' Williams-Ellis and other architects including Sir Robert Lorimer designed some of the first of the ancillary buildings. At first most of these were well integrated with the house and its landscape, but Williams-Ellis's Chatham House (1924–5) introduced a discordant style and material (red brick) into the views from the Rotondo and Temple of Venus, and the building of the school chapel to Lorimer's designs in 1928 involved the demolition of Vanbrugh's Temple of Bacchus. Worse, the chapel itself incorporated eighteenth-century fittings removed from the chapel in the house, and sixteen of the Ionic columns from the peristyle of the Temple of Concord and Victory (see p. 47).

But against this can be set the repairs undertaken from an early stage in the school's history to other garden buildings, notably the Queen's Temple, which was restored in 1933–4 under Fielding Dodd (with donations from the first generation of Old Stoics) and became part of the Music Department. In the course of the 1950s and 1960s the school carried out repairs to ten further buildings and monuments, including the Cobham Monument after it had been struck by lightning in 1957. The Gothic Temple and the eastern Boycott Pavilion became habitable, the former as one of the projects of the Landmark Trust.

The school had single-handedly maintained the garden for 30 years before it was officially recognised that the preservation of the Stowe landscape was a national responsibility. In 1954 the newly formed Historic Buildings Council made its first grants for the upkeep of garden buildings, supporting repairs at Stowe and at Castle Howard. In order to raise the funds necessary to match these grants independently of the school's education resources, the Stowe Landscape Committee was re-formed in 1964, with Sir Ralph Verney as its chairman, and included Christopher Hussey, Laurence Whistler, Howard Colvin and Lord Holford. The committee appointed the architect Hugh Creighton to report on the condition of the buildings, and to draw up a ten-year plan for repairs. The aim of the plan, as he put it, was 'emphatically not to restore the buildings to their pristine condition nor attempt to undo the work of 200 years. It is, in general, to make them structurally sound in their present state, to keep out the weather, and to arrest further deterioration.'

In 1967 the governors entered into a restrictive covenant with the National Trust in order to secure the long-term future of the core of the garden. The replanting of the avenues and other historic plantings was begun with the help of John Workman, the National Trust's Forestry Adviser, and much of the practical work was undertaken by schoolboys supervised by George Clarke, who taught at Stowe from 1950 until 1985, and whose research with Michael Gibbon into the history of Stowe was published in a series of definitive articles in the school magazine, *The Stoic*, from 1967 to 1977.

However, when Creighton prepared a second report in 1983, it became clear that the rate at which the Landscape Committee had been able to carry out repairs was far outstripped by the pace of dilapidation. Simply to make holding repairs to three of the buildings, the Temple of Ancient Virtue, the Corinthian Arch and the Temple of Concord, all of which had received attention in the past 20 years, now required expenditure of £600,000. In 1986 a group of Old Stoics promoted the formation of a new body, the Stowe Garden Buildings Trust, in order to raise the necessary funds, but to many the preservation of Lord Cobham's creation had come to seem an impossible task.

The possibility that the National Trust could extend its role at Stowe emerged in 1989, when an anonymous benefactor offered to contribute £1.8 million, if the Trust were to assume ownership of the garden and its buildings. This was swiftly followed by offers of support from English Heritage and the National Heritage Memorial Fund, and the governors formally conveyed the garden to the National Trust in 1990. For the first time since 1848 it has within a short time become possible to plan a comprehensive restoration of the garden and its buildings, and with the provision of an endowment by the NHMF the long-term future of the landscape seems secure.

The National Trust's first task as owners was to carry out a thorough survey so that restoration could be planned on a proper basis. Individual trees, woodland boundaries, built structures, contours, roads and paths, fences, lakes and streams were plotted on an overall plan; to this were added an inventory of woody plants, an assessment of biological interest, and an archaeological survey, which identified more than 90 'sites' within the garden (including the 32 standing buildings).

The Stowe papers, preserved in the Huntington Library in California, are being examined under the guidance of George Clarke, who was appointed Chairman of the Advisory Committee jointly constituted by the school and the National Trust to

By the late 1980s the Temple of Concord and Victory required urgent attention

direct the restoration. Data from the 350,000 original documents at the Huntington is stored on a computer database so that details of the construction and subsequent repair of each building can be retrieved.

Based on the results of the survey compiled by its Gardens Adviser, Mike Calnan, the Trust has devised a conservation plan in which the objectives for the restoration are set out. The first principle to have been adopted is to ensure the preservation of built or planted features that were meant as additions to the design, leaving the future of others to be decided on their merits. Another is the perpetuation of the main views and axes, which have not essentially changed since 1800. Gardens are continuously changing processes rather than static objects, and any attempt to freeze the Stowe landscape at a particular date would fail, but it has been found that very little of what survives today was begun after the garden and park were accurately mapped in 1843. This huge map is therefore of considerable importance in assessing the form of a plantation or the course of a path. In general, alterations up to this period are being conserved, but in some instances, where areas of the garden matured earlier, restoration will recapture the style of that time.

The extent to which nature had begun to triumph over art was nowhere more evident than in the condition of the lakes, and their clearance was the Trust's first large-scale operation. It had become possible to walk in places across what were originally wide stretches of water. Under the head gardener Frank Thomson, the Alder River and Worthies River, the Octagon Lake and Palladian River, the Eleven-Acre and Copper-Bottom lakes, and finally the Oxford Water were dredged, yielding a total of 320,000 tonnes of silt.

The problem of over-mature trees is often encountered in the restoration of old gardens; at Stowe there is a mixture of ages with the smallest proportion surviving from the eighteenth century, above all because of the 3rd Duke's need to maximise his income from timber. Since 1989 the Trust has felled a number of commercial softwood plantings (for instance, a spruce plantation obscuring the site of the Saxon Deities), thinned other areas, and replanted 20,000 trees and shrubs. A nursery has been established at Dadford in which most species of plants (or their modern equivalents) described in the accounts and by early visitors are propagated and grown on. The re-establishment of paths combines archaeology with the study of plans. In the first few years of the project these were surfaced with chippings from the woodland thinnings, but more recently with gravel dug from the Stowe pits. The National Trust employs just six full-time gardeners, but with the addition of volunteers and those employed on government training schemes, the numbers working in the garden has sometimes approached ducal levels.

The removal of almost all of the statuary from the garden in 1848 and 1921–2 (well over a hundred pieces) stripped away the complex meanings and associations so carefully devised by Lord Cobham. However, with the encouragement and co-opera-tion of their present owners, the Trust has begun to reintroduce many of the statues in the form of casts. Copies of the four Virtuous Greeks have thus been returned to their niches in the Temple of Ancient Virtue, and, excepting Thuner, the circle of the Saxon Deities has been re-assembled in the Wick Quarter.

The condition of the garden buildings was re-assessed in 1989–90 by Peter Inskip, who then proposed a sequence of campaigns of repair. Their condition varies but almost all of them require attention, and temporary scaffolding will be seen in the garden for many years to come. The Trust's fundamental policy is to conserve as much as possible of the original fabric of each temple or monument. Holding works have been carried out to the Temple of Friendship, the Palladian Bridge and the Grotto, together with small 'trial' contracts to the Bell Gate and Hermitage, intended to establish the best materials and methods for use on the remaining buildings. The largest tasks so far have been the repairs to the Grenville Column, the Temple of Ancient Virtue, the Oxford Gates and Lodges and the Temples of Venus and Concord and Victory, the Rotunda and Dido's Cave, Lord Cobham's Pillar and the Fane of Pastoral Poetry, General Wolfe's Obelisk, Conduit House and the Lake Pavilions.

The roof of the Temple of Ancient Virtue was found to be bearing unequally on the Ionic peristyle, and the surrounding ground levels were much altered. A concrete ring beam now supports the dome, and the renders have been completed using the constituents of the original material.

Kent's original domes to the pavilions of the Temple of Venus had already subsided by 1827–8, when the 1st Duke of Buckingham replaced them with pitched lead roofs. At about the same time the door openings were enlarged, the south-facing windows blocked up and what was left of the original decoration obscured by new paint. In the present century the coved ceiling collapsed and was removed. Faced with so severely damaged a building, the Stowe Advisory Committee approved a proposal to restore as much of Kent's original design as could reliably be reconstructed. Sadly, this could not include Sleter's murals, of which only a single hand and part of the branch of a tree survived.

*The Temple of Concord
and Victory after its
recent restoration*

The Temple of Concord had been on Death Row for decades, and by the early 1980s there seemed little point in spending anything further on keeping the roof watertight. However, with the renewed commitment of English Heritage and the assistance of private benefactors it has recently been possible to reroof the building entirely, to carve and reinstate sixteen new columns (the originals remain in Lorimer's chapel, which is itself now a listed building), to restore the interior and the stucco of the external walls, and to reinstate sculpture to the roof, at a cost of £1.3 million.

In 1995 the National Trust was able to purchase the 320 acres of the Home Farm which lie immediately to the north of the garden, with the help of funds from the National Lottery distributed by the Heritage Lottery Fund (see p. 56). Further afield, the Trust is collaborating with neighbouring landowners in an informal Freeholders' Association for the long-term protection of the Stowe landscape.

CHAPTER TEN

THE FAME OF STOWE

Pope called Stowe 'a work to wonder at'. Like most eighteenth-century visitors, he was impressed by the size, splendour and variety of the gardens and their unusual abundance of ornamental buildings – 'decorations', remarked the Swedish garden architect F. M. Piper in 1779, 'of a dimension, size and variety that betray a desire to gain renown and to exceed all others in point of expense and magnitude'. Stowe was a microcosm of landscape and building, and was, asserted Thomas Whately in 1770, 'like one of those places celebrated in antiquity ... the resort of distant nations and the object of veneration to half the heathen world'.

Despite Stowe's immense popularity, it is difficult to calculate the extent of the garden's influence, and to differentiate it from that of other important English landscape gardens of the day. Claremont, Richmond, Chiswick and Stourhead all

had features in common with Stowe, and several smaller gardens, such as Woburn Farm, Painshill and The Leasowes, approached it in influence and reputation. However, with the exception of Kew, no other English garden of the eighteenth century could rival the number, scale and complex iconography of the ornamental garden buildings at Stowe. Moreover, many of these structures were by celebrated architects, giving Stowe a distinct architectural emphasis, which often overshadowed the significance of the landscape and planting.

Soon after Lord Cobham began work on the gardens, he opened them to the curious, building the New Inn on the margins of the garden in 1717 to accommodate visitors. Stowe was also the subject of the first guidebook to any country house garden in England (see p. 95). Public curiosity was fuelled further by other publications – poetic trib-

Victoria and Albert passing beneath the Corinthian Arch on their visit to Stowe in 1845

utes such as Gilbert West's *Stowe* (1732) or prose descriptions like those found in Samuel Richardson's edition of Defoe's *A Tour thro' the Whole Island of Great Britain* (1742).

From 1750 these published descriptions were supplemented by illustrations of the gardens, although they were by no means always accurate or up-to-date. Cobham's formal gardens were known from a handsome series of engraved views by Jacques Rigaud, published in 1739, but they had been drawn in 1733–4 and depicted only its formal 'Bridgmannick' elements and none of Kent's Arcadian incursions. Even the crude 'cuts' of the garden buildings from Seeley and Bickham's guidebooks showed little of their landscape context. Stowe was never the subject of a serious architectural publication like Sir William Chambers's *Plans ... of the Gardens and Buildings at Kew* (1763) and perhaps even more regrettably, none of Nattes's watercolour views of the gardens at around their zenith in 1805–9 was ever engraved.

The fame of Stowe was well established by 1724, having 'already gained the reputation of the finest seat in England'. Even at this early date, it was unrivalled for its unusual garden buildings, some of which were imitated elsewhere. Vanbrugh's Rotondo (1720–1) was copied at Hall Barn (1725) and at Studley Royal (c.1728–32). His Pyramid (1724; now gone) inspired similar structures at Tring (c.1725) and Castle Howard (1728; both also gone). No less influential than the buildings was Bridgeman's ha-ha (see p. 13), a feature found in almost all large landscape gardens later in the century.

Cobham's 'garden of exile' (see p. 6) has affinities with those which consoled other outcasts, notably the Tory Earl Bathurst at Cirencester Park (from 1714), the disgraced financier John Aislabie at Studley Royal (1720–42) and the superannuated General Dormer at Rousham (from 1737). Between 1739 and 1791 at the rival Yorkshire estates of Wentworth Castle and Wentworth Woodhouse an astonishing series of garden structures – lookout towers, columns and obelisks – commemorated the divided political allegiances of the estranged branches of one family. In an echo of the Temple of British Worthies, Frederick, Prince of Wales set up busts of King Alfred and the Black Prince in his

A

DESCRIPTION

OF THE

GARDENS

OF

Lord Viſcount COBHAM,

AT

STOW in BUCKINGHAMSHIRE.

Here Order in Variety you ſee,
Where all Things differ, ---- yet where all agree !
A. POPE.

NORTHAMPTON:
Printed by W. DICEY ; and ſold by B. *Seeley*, Writing-Maſter, in *Buckingham*, and *George Norris*, Peruke-Maker, in *Newport-Pagnell, Bucks.* M.DCC.XLIV.

The title-page from the first, 1744, edition of Benton Seeley's Stowe guidebook, which helped to spread the fame of the gardens

garden at Carlton House. He also planned a 'Mount Parnassus' for Kew on the model of the Elysian Fields, but died before it could be completed.

Stowe's Arcadia intrigued rather than inspired most visitors. Nothing came of an anonymous proposal of c.1735 to remodel the gardens at Bovingdon House in Devon with a whole series of monuments borrowed from Stowe, including a 'Dormitory', a 'Temple of the Worthies' and an 'Altar of the Saxon Gods'. Lord Petre's unexecuted 1738 design for an ambitious garden for the Duke of Norfolk at Worksop contained a Rotunda, a Temple of Ancient Virtue and a Palladian Bridge, as well as a monster *exedra* doubtless derived from the Temple of British Worthies. Curiously, the most daring

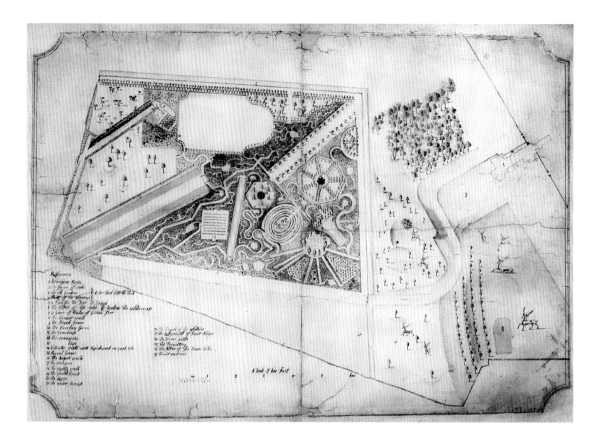

*An anonymous design for a garden at Boringdon House,
Devon, c.1735 – a provincial response to Stowe*

novelties erected at Stowe in the 1730 and '40s were
also isolated phenomena. The Chinese House
(*c*.1738) was one of the first Chinoiserie garden
buildings in this country, but had little influence on
the next wave of Chinese structures, at Old Windsor, Shugborough and Kew. The most ambitious of
all early Gothick garden buildings, the triangular
Gothic Temple, had no close imitators.

Perhaps Stowe's most influential creation was
'Capability' Brown, who perfected his art and made
his reputation there between 1741 and 1751. Subsequently, he worked on innumerable landscape
gardens up and down the country, often being
called upon to 'naturalise' earlier formal layouts,
much as he had done at Stowe.

Many of the 'sacred landscapes' created by
Brown and his followers in the second half of the

eighteenth century can be compared to Stowe,
including the temple-strewn gardens of West
Wycombe and Wentworth Woodhouse. Indeed, it
has recently been suggested that Sir Francis Dash-
wood planned features of West Wycombe in
parody of his old enemy's gardens at Stowe. Friend-
lier, family ties resulted in close parallels between
Stowe and Hagley, the garden made by Lord
Cobham's nephew, George Lyttelton. Almost
every feature at Hagley had a precursor at Stowe:
the 'Grecian Temple' (1747; now the Temple of
Concord and Victory) had a counterpart in Stuart's
Temple of Theseus at Hagley (1758); Cobham's
columns topped with statues of the Prince and
Princess of Wales were answered by a similar
column at Hagley, and both Stowe and Hagley had
an Ionic Rotunda and a Palladian Bridge. Stowe
Castle (before 1738) and the Keeper's Lodge
(*c*.1741; now the Bourbon Tower) prefigured
Hagley's Ruined Castle (1747). However, Lyttelton

was also advised by William Shenstone of The Leasowes, and his gardens had a 'savage' aspect akin to the Picturesque landscapes of Hawkstone and Hackfall. Many gardens which appear to be influenced by Stowe are in fact indebted to its rivals.

Temple's purification of the gardens and the increasing maturity of Cobham's plantations left Stowe at the height of its splendour and reputation. Yet because Temple primarily patronised foreign architects or sought advice from one of his aristocratic kinsmen, none of whom carried out much work elsewhere, Stowe was somewhat isolated architecturally. His ambitious plans for two grand commemorative buildings, a Mausoleum and a Rotunda, remained unrealised, although they may have influenced a contemporary political Valhalla at Wentworth Woodhouse, known as the Rockingham Mausoleum.

Distant echoes of Stowe can be found in countless gardens throughout northern Europe, but again

direct links are curiously difficult to find. The French were particularly fascinated by Stowe, which was illustrated in George Le Rouge's *Détails de nouveaux jardins à la mode* (1776–88). Moreover, many Frenchmen came to see Stowe for themselves, descending on the gardens in such numbers that a guidebook entitled *Les Charmes de Stow* was brought out in 1748.

An evocation of Stowe can be found at the Parc Monceau, a celebrated *jardin anglais* laid out in 1773–8 for the Anglophile duc de Chartres. Monceau was frequently compared to Stowe by French commentators and contained 'a quantity of curious things' – a minaret, pyramid, wood of tombs, Italian vineyard, military column, Turkish tent and a water-mill. However, it was also very like Kew and Painshill.

Reminders of Stowe occur in other French gardens of the period. At the Désert de Retz, François Racine de Monville created, from 1774, an extra-

'The Wood of Tombs', in the Parc Monceau – the 'French Stowe' (Musée Carnavalet, Paris)

ordinary garden surrounding a house in the form of a shattered column, with exotic buildings like a Chinese house, a pyramid and a Gothic chapel. At Betz, designed by Hubert Robert and the duc d'Harcoult for the princesse de Monaco, the very names of the buildings – the Temple of Friendship and the Pavilion of Rest – suggest a conscious imitation of specific models from Stowe. Méréville, laid out from 1784 by F. J. Bélanger (who had visited England in 1777–8 and made drawings of Stowe) and Hubert Robert for the duc de Laborde, had a towering 'Colonne Triumphale', a monument to Captain Cook, and a peripteral temple resembling the Temple of Ancient Virtue. Other examples of the French mania for *jardins anglais* include those at Rambouillet, Bagatelle, Mauperthuis and around the Petit Trianon at Versailles, and, in perhaps its most extravagant and eccentric form, the gardens of the Folie Saint-James at Neuilly. Luxurious and 'loaded with incoherent and useless ornaments', almost all these gardens fell victim, like their owners, to the French Revolution.

In Germany the taste for English landscape gardens was taken up with perhaps even more enthusiasm than in France, thanks to influential publications such as C. C. L. Hirschfeld's *Theorie der Gartenkunst* (1779–85). In the 1760s Prince Franz von Anhalt-Dessau, accompanied by his architect and his gardener, made two visits to England and saw many important gardens, including Stowe. His gardens at Wörlitz, near Dessau, begun in 1770 and successively extended until 1800, contain more garden buildings than Stowe, including a synagogue, a Gothic house and a volcano, but none directly relates to structures at Stowe, and features like the *Rousseau-Insel* betray a clear debt to Ermenonville. A somewhat generalised English inspiration can be seen in the countless German landscape gardens of the second half of the eighteenth century, like those at Schwetzingen, remodelled for the Grand Duke of Baden from 1774 by Freidrich Ludwig von Sckell (who had studied in England), or Hohenheim, near Stuttgart.

In Sweden the English landscape manner was introduced by F. M. Piper, who had visited England in the 1770s and made drawings of Stowe and other English landscape gardens for his unpublished *Idea and Plan for an English Pleasure Park*. Piper subsequently promoted his ideas at a number of Swedish landscape gardens, including those at Drottningholm and Haga. Gardens on the English model are also found in Hungary, notably in those laid out for members of the Esterházy family at Csákvár (1781–1800), Tata (from 1784) and Kismarton (from 1801). In Poland the style was promoted by the King, Stanislas Poniatowski, who had visited Stowe in 1754, and is exemplified by the garden-retreat of Arkadia, created by Princess Helena Radziwill and her architect Szymon Bogumił Zug.

But Stowe's greatest admirer was the Empress Catherine the Great of Russia, who was fascinated with English landscape gardens and sent her gardener Vasily Neelov to England in 1770–1 to 'visit all the notable gardens and, having seen them, lay out similar ones here'. Neelov almost certainly saw Stowe during his six months' sojourn in England and spent the rest of his life recasting her pleasure grounds at Tsarskoe Selo and Peterhof in the English style. The former contains a sequence of Palladian Bridge, rostral column, Corinthian Arch and pyramid all directly derived from Stowe. The 'Stoic' monuments at Tsarskoe Selo together comprise perhaps the most complete and studied evocation of the gardens anywhere. Unable to visit Stowe herself, the Empress was constantly reminded of the gardens and their significance: the celebrated Frog Service, commissioned by her from Wedgwood in 1773, has more views of Stowe than of any other garden.

Although southern Europe remained largely unaffected by the craze for English landscape gardens in the eighteenth century, the style was promoted in Italy in the early nineteenth century by Count Ercole Silva, author of *Dell' arte dei giardini inglesi* (1813), whose own gardens at Cinisello in Lombardy were described as 'the Leasowes or Stow of the Milanese'. Stowe found admirers across the Atlantic: Thomas Jefferson went to Stowe in 1786 and recalled it in his own garden at Monticello.

In the nineteenth century the gardens at Stowe gradually sank into decline, and contemporary opinion often echoed Prince Pückler-Muskau's criticisms (see p. 79). Curiously, the very surfeit of ornaments he complained about became a characteristic of the grandest private and public pleasure

Bird's-eye view of the gardens of 'The Palace of Malplaquet' – a fictional Stowe – drawn by Raymond McGrath for the endpapers of T. H. White's Mistress Masham's Repose *(1947)*

grounds laid out later in the century. Comparison can be made between Stowe and the gardens Joseph Paxton designed for the Crystal Palace after it was moved to Sydenham, with their mixture of formal and informal elements and a host of novelties lurking in the shrubberies.

Denuded of its statuary by the sales of 1848 and 1921–2, in its ruin Stowe has exerted perhaps a greater fascination than at any time in its history. The pleasing effects of time on the buildings and full splendour of the overgrown planting coincided with a revival of appreciation of eighteenth-century architecture and landscape gardens. Despite its incongruity, the occupation of the great palace and

its pleasure grounds by Stowe School has doubtless ensured its preservation far more effectively than had they remained in private ownership. Certainly, the gardens, with their tangled undergrowth and decaying temples pressed into service as classrooms, boat-houses and tuck-shops, had a potent influence on generations of young Stoics. Many may even regret the passing of their forlorn grandeur, celebrated in the paintings of John Piper and the photographs of Osvald Siren. The derelict gardens are also brilliantly evoked (as those of the fictional Malplaquet Palace) in T. H. White's novel, *Mistress Masham's Repose* (1947), and permeate the work of Rex and Laurence Whistler, the latter an Old Stoic. There is no twentieth-century equivalent to Stowe, although in recent times the influence of this decayed Arcadia can perhaps be found in the modern garden of inscriptions created by Ian Hamilton Finlay at Little Sparta.

THE OWNERS OF STOWE

Owners of Stowe are in CAPITALS

* 'Cobham's Cubs' (see. p.65)

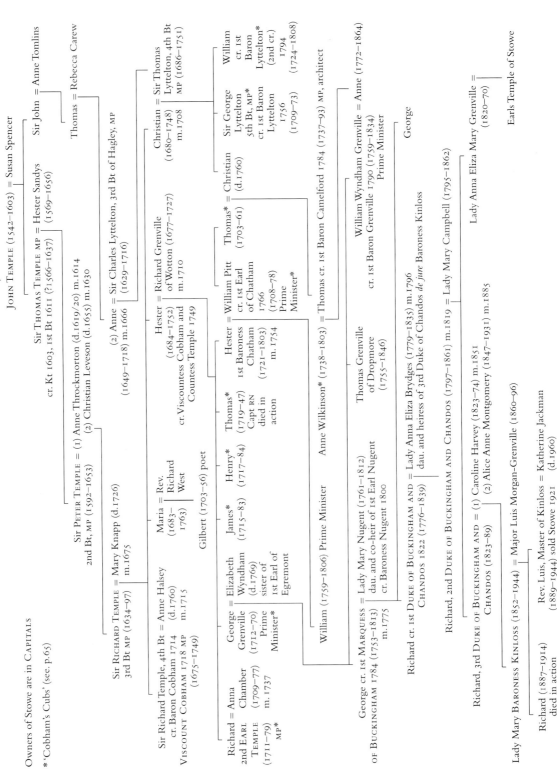

BIBLIOGRAPHY

UNPUBLISHED AND VISUAL SOURCES

The Stowe papers in the Henry E. Huntington Library, San Marino, California, which include 350,000 documents, provide an unrivalled level of detailed information on the history of the garden. Likewise, the visual sources are more numerous than for any other English garden. As well as the illustrations to the guidebooks, amateur drawings and photographs, two systematic records were made: the set of fifteen views by Jacques Rigaud commissioned by Charles Bridgeman and published in 1739, and 105 wash drawings of the house and gardens by John Claude Nattes made in 1805–9.

GUIDEBOOKS

The compiler of a modern guide to the gardens at Stowe must take account of an exceptionally long tradition, and in the process add to it. *A Description of the Gardens of Lord Viscount Cobham at Stow in Buckinghamshire*, largely based on the description in the 1742 edition of Daniel Defoe and Samuel Richardson's *A Tour thro' the Whole Island of Great Britain*, was published by Benton Seeley, a writing-master, in 1744. It was the first guide to a country seat published in England for the general reader or tourist, and found a ready market. New editions were printed in successive years until 1749, and Seeley brought out two 'companion' volumes, William Gilpin's *A Dialogue upon the Gardens at Stow* and a set of *Views of the Temples and other Ornamental Buildings in the Gardens at Stow* in 1748 and 1750. In the latter year the topographical engraver George Bickham published in London *The Beauties of Stow*, a pirated conflation of all three of Seeley's books, with new illustrations. Competition led both publishers towards wider distribution and further refinements such as maps. Eventually Seeley prevailed and his guides continued to be printed until 1827. In the present century the tradition has been extended by Laurence Whistler, Michael Gibbon and George Clarke's *Stowe: A Guide to the Gardens*, first published in 1956 and revised in 1968 and 1974. For the bibliography of the early guides, see John Harris's *A Country House Index* (1977) and Clarke's introduction to the 1977 facsimile of Bickham's *The Beauties of Stow*.

ADDISON, Joseph, 'A Continuation of the Vision', *The Tatler*, no. 123, 21 January 1709.

ANNAN, Noel, *Roxburgh of Stowe*, London, 1965.

BECKETT, John V., *The Rise and Fall of the Grenvilles*, Manchester, 1994.

BEVINGTON, Michael, 'The Development of the Classical Revival at Stowe', *Architectura*, xxi, no. 2, 1991, pp. 136–63.
Templa Quam Dilecta, nos 1–13, 1989.
Stowe: A Guide to the House, Stowe, 1990.
Stowe: The Garden and Park, 2nd ed., Stowe, 1995.

BIRDWOOD, Vere, ed., *So dearly loved, so much admired: Letters to Hester Pitt, Lady Chatham ...*, London, 1994.

BOYSE, Samuel, 'The Triumphs of Nature: A Poem on the Magnificent Gardens at Stowe in Buckinghamshire, the Seat of the Rt. Hon. Lord Cobham', *Gentleman's Magazine*, xii, June 1742, p. 234, July, pp. 380–2, August, pp. 435–6 (repr. in Clarke 1990, pp. 94–100).

BRIDGEMAN, Sarah , *General Plan of the Woods, Park and Gardens of Stowe, with Several Perspective Views in the Garden*, Thomas Bowles, 1746.

BUCKINGHAM AND CHANDOS, Richard Temple-Nugent-Brydges-Chandos-Grenville, 1st Duke of, *Private Diary*, i–iii, Hurst and Blackett, 1862.

BURRELL, Michael and Innis, *The Temple of British Worthies: An Illustrated Guide*, 1983.

CHATELAIN, J. B., *Sixteen Perspective Views, together with a General Plan of the ... Buildings and Gardens at Stowe ... drawn on the Spot 1752, engraved by George Bickham junior*, 1752.

CHRISTIE & MANSON, *Catalogue of the Contents of Stowe, near Buckingham (Seat of the Duke of Buckingham & Chandos) which will be sold by auction by Messrs Christie & Manson*, William Clowes [1848].

CLARKE, George B., and GIBBON, Michael J., 'The History of Stowe', *The Stoic*, i–xxvi, 1967–77.

CLARKE, George B., 'The Early Gardens at Stowe (for Sir Richard Temple, 1679–1697)', *Country Life*, cxlv, 2 January 1969, pp. 6–9.
'Military Gardening at Stowe', *Country Life*, cli, 18 May 1972, pp. 1254–6.
'William Kent, Heresy in Stowe's Elysium', in Peter Willis, ed., *Furor Hortensis*, 1973, pp. 48–56.
'The Gardens of Stowe', *Apollo*, xcvii, June 1973, pp. 558–65.
'Grecian Taste and Gothic Virtue: Lord Cobham's Gardening Programme and its Iconography', *Apollo*, xcvii, June 1973, pp. 566–71.
'The Medallions of Concord: An Association between the Society of Arts and Stowe', *Journal of the Royal Society of Arts*, cxxix, August 1981, pp. 611–6.
'Where did all the Trees come from? An Analysis of Bridgeman's Planting at Stowe', *Journal of Garden History*, v, January/March 1985, pp. 72–83.

'Signor Fido and the Stowe Patriots', *Apollo*, cxxii, October 1985, pp. 248–51.

ed., *Descriptions of Lord Cobham's Gardens at Stowe, 1700–1750*, Buckinghamshire Record Society, 1990.

'The Moving Temples of Stowe: Aesthetics of Change in an English Landscape over Four Generations', *Huntington Library Quarterly*, lv, 1992, pp. 479–532.

CORNFORTH, John, 'Achievement and Challenge: The Preservation of the Stowe Landscape', *Country Life*, clxxix, 24 April 1986, pp. 1108–10.

CREIGHTON, Hugh, 'Repairs to the Garden Buildings at Stowe', *The Stoic*, March 1967, p. 206.

FITZGERALD, Desmond, 'History of the Interior of Stowe', *Apollo*, lxxvii, June 1973, pp. 572–85.

FORSTER, Henry Rumsey, ed., *The Stowe Catalogue priced and annotated . . . sale . . . entrusted to Messrs Christie and Manson etc.*, David Bogue, 1848.

GIBBON, Michael J., 'A Forgotten Italian at Stowe: Vincenzo Valdre, Architect and Painter', *Country Life*, cxl, 4 August 1966, pp. 260–3.

'The Queen's Temple at Stowe', *Country Life*, cxlv, 9 January 1969, pp. 78–80.

'Manifesto in Ironstone: The Gothic Temple at Stowe', *Country Life*, cli, 1 June 1972, pp. 1416–17.

'Stowe House, 1680–1779', *Apollo*, xcvii, June 1973, pp. 552–7.

'The First Neo-classical Building? Temple of Concord, Stowe', *Country Life*, clv, 11 April 1974, pp. 852–3.

'Stowe, Buckinghamshire: The House and Garden Buildings and their Designers: A Catalogue', *Architectural History*, xx, 1977, pp. 31–44; with George Clarke, 'Addenda to Stowe', xxi, 1978, p. 93.

HALL, Michael, 'Stowe Landscape Gardens I & II', *Country Life*, 22, 29 February 1996.

HARRIS, John, 'Blondel at Stowe', *Connoisseur*, clv, March 1964, pp. 173–6.

HAYDEN, Peter, 'British Seats on Imperial Russian Tables', *Garden History*, xiii, no. 1, 1985, pp. 17–32.

'The Russian Stowe: Benton Seeley's Guidebooks as a Source of Catherine the Great's Park at Tsarskoe Selo', *Garden History*, xix, no. 1, spring 1991, pp. 21–7.

HUSSEY, Christopher, 'Stowe, Buckinghamshire: 1. The Connection of Georgian Landscape with Whig Politics', *Country Life*, cii, 12 September 1947, pp. 526–9; '2. Rhetoric in Landscape Architecture', 19 September 1947, pp. 578–81; '3. Heroic Phase', 26 September 1947, pp. 626–9.

English Landscape Gardens, 1967, pp. 89–113.

INSKIP, Peter, 'Discoveries, Challenges and Moral Dilemmas in the Restoration of the Garden Buildings at Stowe', *Huntington Library Quarterly*, lv, 1992, pp. 511–26.

JACKSON-STOPS (Auctioneers), *The Ducal Estate at Stowe*, Towcester, 1921, 1922.

JACKSON-STOPS, Gervase, *An English Arcadia 1600–1990*, 1991.

'Sharawadgi Rediscovered: The Chinese House at Stowe', *Apollo*, cxxxvii, no. 374, April 1993, pp. 217–22.

KENWORTHY-BROWNE, John, 'Rysbrack's Saxon Deities', *Apollo*, cxxii, September 1985, pp. 220–7.

LIPSCOMB, George, *The History and Antiquities of the County of Buckingham*, iii, 1843, pp. 84–108.

MCCARTHY, Michael, 'Eighteenth Century Amateur Architects and their Gardens', in Nikolaus Pevsner, ed., *The Picturesque Garden & its Influence outside the British Isles*, pp. 31–55.

'James Lovell and his Sculptures at Stowe', *Burlington Magazine*, cxv, no. 841, April 1973, pp. 221–32.

'The Rebuilding of Stowe House, 1770–1777', *Huntington Library Quarterley*, xxxvi, no. 3, 1973, pp. 267–89.

MOORE, Susan, 'Hail! Gods of our Fore-fathers: Rysbrack's "Lost" Saxon Deities at Stowe', *Country Life*, 31 January 1985.

ROBINSON, John Martin, *Temples of Delight: Stowe Landscape Gardens*, 1990.

SHEAHAN, James Joseph, *History and Topography of Buckinghamshire*, 1862.

THOMPSON, F. M. L., 'The end of a great estate', *Economic History Review*, 2nd ser., viii, 1 August 1955, pp. 36–52.

WEST, Gilbert, *Stowe*, 1732 (repr. in Clarke, 1990, pp. 36–51).

WHATELY, Thomas, *Observations on Modern Gardening*, Dublin, 1770.

WHEELER, Richard W., 'The Park and Garden Survey at Stowe: The Replanting and Restoration of the Historical Landscape', *Huntington Library Quarterly*, lv, 1992, pp. 527–32).

'The Gardens of Stowe and West Wycombe: Paradise and Parody?', *Apollo*, cxlv, April 1997, pp. 3–7.

WHISTLER, Laurence, 'The Authorship of Stowe Temples', *Country Life*, cviii, 29 September 1950, pp. 1002–6.

The Imagination of Vanbrugh and his Fellow Artists, 1954.

'Signor Borra at Stowe, *Country Life*, cxxii, 29 August 1957, pp. 390–3.

Stowe: A Guide to the Gardens, 1956, 2nd rev. ed. by Laurence Whistler, Michael Gibbon and George Clarke, Buckingham, 1968; 3rd rev. ed. 1974.

WHITE, T. H., *Mistress Masham's Repose*, London, 1947.

WHITFIELD, Paul, 'Bankruptcy and Sale at Stowe: 1848', *Apollo*, xcvii, June 1973, pp. 599–604.

WHITWELL, Stephen, 'Expelled to Stowe: the Comte de Paris in Exile', *Country Life*, clxxxiii, 7 December 1989, pp. 180–6.

WILLIAMS-ELLIS, Clough, 'Stowe, Past and Future', *The Spectator*, cxxvii, 23 July 1921, p. 103.

WILLIS, Peter, 'From Desert to Eden: Charles Bridgeman's "Capital Stroke"', *Burlington Magazine*, cxv, no. 840, March 1973, pp. 150–7.

Charles Bridgeman and the English Landscape Garden, 1977, pp. 106–27.

WOODBRIDGE, Kenneth, 'William Kent as Landscape Gardener: A Re-appraisal', *Apollo*, c, 1974, pp. 126–37.